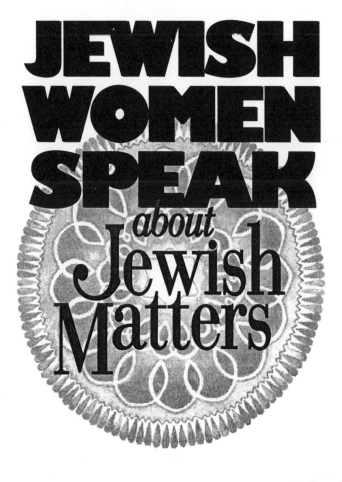

JEWISH WOMEN SPEAK *about* Jewish Matters

JEWISH WOMEN SPEAK

about Jewish Matters

Edited by
Sarah Tikvah Kornbluth
and Doron Kornbluth

TARGUM/FELDHEIM
in conjunction with
CONTINUITY PRESS

First published 2000
Copyright © 2000 by Doron Kornbluth
ISBN 1-56871-151-4

Published by:
Targum Press, Inc.
22700 W. Eleven Mile Rd.
Southfield, MI 48034
targum@netvision.net.il
fax: 888-298-9992

in conjuction with:
Continuity Press

Distributed by:
Feldheim Publishers
200 Airport Executive Park
Nanuet, NY 10954
www.feldheim.com
Printed in Israel

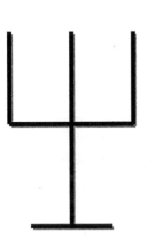

In memory of

Bertha G. Rothman

Rose R. Amster

Charlotte Rothman

Helene R. Lefko

Golde N. Rothman

*Women of valor who
built their homes with wisdom*

Published through the courtesy of the
HENRY, BERTHA, and EDWARD ROTHMAN FOUNDATION
Rochester, N.Y. • Circleville, Ohio • Cleveland

Contents

Speaking about...Jewish Women, Present

Speaking about...Gender and Roles

Speaking about...Biblical Texts

Acknowledgments

Over two years ago we embarked on a project that came to be called *Jewish Matters: A Pocketbook of Knowledge and Inspiration*. Feeling a lack of small, user-friendly books to inform and inspire young and not-so-young Jews about their heritage, we gathered essays by many of the most respected male and female teachers of Jewish ideas from around the world for what we hoped would be a light, positive, but powerful anthology.

Our hopes were realized, and *Jewish Matters* has been warmly received by people hailing from all over the wide spectrum of Jewish backgrounds. From summer programs to federations to the friend at the office who is always asking questions, one little book has found a big niche. Available on Amazon.com and in selected Barnes and Nobles, Steimatzky (Israel's national bookstore chain), and Jewish bookstores around the world, *Jewish Matters* is starting to find itself in more and more Jewish homes.

In the many warm comments we received about *Jewish Matters*, one subject kept coming up: women's issues. It became clear that whatever personal path readers were interested in, the impression that classical Jewish tradition looks down at women is one of the biggest obstacles to many Jews feeling close to their heritage. We have therefore put together *Jewish Women*

Speak about Jewish Matters in order to, hopefully, break down this stereotype and inspire Jewish women about their identities as Jewish women.

Jewish Women Speak is similar in style to the first book in the series, with a few unique features. All contributors are women. Although we firmly believe that men have the right to speak about women's issues, because, after all, one must evaluate messages irrespective of the messengers that bring them, still, often women can speak to other women more effectively than men can.

Also, unlike the first volume, which dealt with a huge variety of subjects and themes relevant to Jewish people today, this volume deals solely with subjects that revolve around the value, importance, contributions, and personal journeys of Jewish women. This doesn't mean that only women should read it — sometimes men need this information more than women do!

Three notes to the reader: First, in this one anthology we have not even attempted to cover every area necessary to gaining a full understanding of what it means to be a Jewish woman. The subject is simply too vast. While many important related areas are dealt with, others are not touched on at all, or only barely. The explanation for this lies in our space limitations, the difficulty of covering complex subjects in a few pages, and the conviction that the principles that are dealt with in *Jewish Women Speak* should give the understanding reader insights into areas that are not dealt with.

Furthermore, we encourage the curious reader to look into the many works of our contributors to further explore questions and areas of interest they have. Simply put, *Jewish Women Speak* is not meant to answer or even address all the issues surrounding the subject of Jewish women and the Jewish tradition — our goal is to inform, inspire, and encourage further study and reflection.

Second, no area of Jewish philosophy or outlook can

be properly understood if looked at in a vacuum. Jewish life and outlook form a beautiful, integrated whole. In this vein, as central as women's issues are — as they should be — to fully understand the subject, one must have a good understanding of other aspects of our heritage as well. To this end, we cannot help but recommend our *Jewish Matters: A Pocketbook of Knowledge and Inspiration* as an easy, user-friendly introduction to subjects ranging from relationships to Shabbat, from prayer to antisemitism, with essays from many of the most respected names in adult Jewish education today. Contributors to that volume have also written some of the best books available on many relevant subjects. Coming soon (we hope!) are small user-friendly *Jewish Matters* books on the Jewish holidays, the Jewish lifecycle, and more.

Third, the personal quotes that appear at the beginning of each section are a combination of direct quotes from Jewish women around the world and paraphrases of memorable quotes women have heard. (Names and other personal information have been changed where appropriate.)

And so, we are honored to present the educators and authors who appear in this volume. Many of them we know personally and are happy to consider our teachers and friends. All of them were most generous with their time and talent to what we all perceive as an important cause: giving all Jews, irrespective of their backgrounds, the opportunity to learn about and fall in love with their heritage.

Without Rabbi Bernard Rothman and everyone else at the Rothman Foundation, it is hard to imagine this book having come together. Their constant support of English-language Jewish books is making a real difference in the survival and revival of the Jewish people and deserves our admiration and thanks.

Rabbi Moshe Dombey, Mrs. Mimi Zakon, Mrs. D. Liff, Mrs. Suri Brand, and the rest of the staff at Targum have been extremely positive and encouraging from the start.

High professional standards matched with a friendly personal touch make Targum a jewel to work with.

Many other people have been of immense help along the way, from critiquing, editing, improving, rewriting, encouraging, vetoing, supporting, and thinking a few steps ahead of us. Andrew Shaw and his team at UJS inspired the first work. David and Talya Roth and their families enabled *Jewish Matters* to get off the ground, and so share in the credit for this volume as well. Elimelekh Lehman's early support helped us see things through. Our good friends Jon and Jessica Erlbaum, Fraidy Josephson, Donna Rader, Dave and Kerry Behrendt, Keren Lynn, Simi Yellin, Bayla Miro, Dina Dorian, Ammi Field, Miriam Ciner, Stephen and Sarah Berger, David and Ali Begoun, Scott and Aliza Kahn, Professor Bill Kollbrener, and many other friends, relatives, and complete strangers were generous with their time in critiquing essays and suggesting improvements. Their help was invaluable. Special thanks to Jonathan and Deana Bressel of the soon-to-be-published *Shabbat Table Guide* for endless advice and encouragement.

Our parents have done so much for us in so many ways that mere words cannot begin to be adequate. Special thanks go to our mothers, Judy Kornbluth and Joy Siegel, for their valuable editing and critiquing. Hardly a word of *Jewish Women Speak* escaped their scrutiny and excellent advice.

And finally, many thanks to all the readers of *Jewish Matters*, whose positive feedback and support were essential to its successor, in your hands now, coming into being.

Sarah Tikvah Kornbluth   Doron Kornbluth

Jerusalem 5760/2000

P.S. For comments, questions, suggestions, or to be in touch with the authors, please contact us at editors@jewishmatters.com or visit us at www.jewishmatters.com.

Foreword

I don't often go to synagogue. Not for a particularly philosophical reason — I just find I can concentrate better when I'm alone. Even when I do go, it is usually on Friday night for the beautiful prayers that welcome Shabbat. Yet it did happen that once, many years ago, I woke up early on a Shabbat morning and decided to attend services.

I got dressed and walked outside, unsure of my destination. As you can imagine, Jerusalem (my home at the time) has no shortage of synagogues. Since I hadn't visited it for quite a while, I decided to go to the Western Wall in the Old City. True, there were crowds and tourists, which could make it hard to concentrate, but it is such a special place that I always walk away with a feeling of peace and connection to my people, my heritage, and, yes, God.

On this particular morning I witnessed something quite extraordinary. As I entered the plaza, a large group of men were escorting a frail old man with a long beard toward the Wall. His dark skin made it obvious to me that he was a Sefardi Jew. In my broken Hebrew, I asked people nearby who the man was. All I could understand from their response was that he was a great rabbi, considered to be a sage and a holy person. I managed to get a glimpse of his face and was taken aback. His bright, piercing eyes were those of child, peering right into me. Instead of going to pray, I positioned myself in a place where I could keep my eye on this special rabbi. He was accorded great respect and given a seat right in front of the Wall, which he kissed and grasped with his hands like an old friend.

The time came for the blessing of the priests. Growing up in Christian countries, we often think of priests in Christian terms, but our tradition includes priests as well. They are known as *kohanim*. In the times of the Temple, they led the services and brought all the offerings and were particularly visible and important. Today, with no Holy Temple in Jerusalem, there are still some special rules that apply to them, for instance, the prohibition of not entering a cemetery and the honor of performing a special blessing in the morning prayer services. In the diaspora, this blessing is pronounced only a few times a year on special holidays, usually with great attention and respect. In Israel, it happens every day.

In the services I was watching at the Wall, it so happened that there were only two *kohanim* present, both young boys whom I recognized as part of the group that had escorted the old rabbi. These were two young boys. They were obviously not much older than bar mitzvah, and yet upon their return, this special old rabbi jumped up to get out of their way and let them stand in front of the congregation. They pronounced the blessing, and then the rabbi rushed up to them, bent over, and kissed their hands. Other congregants did the same thing. Later I learned this is a Sefardic custom to show respect for the *kohanim*. Needless to say, I had never witnessed this before and was quite surprised.

This old, frail rabbi was jumping up and bending over to kiss the hands of boys who were easily seventy years his junior. And they had just an hour before escorted him in, treating him as the one worthy of honor!

What was going on?

And then it hit me. What I had witnessed was not a contradiction. When the *kohanim* were offered respect and honor, it did not mean that they were better than anyone else. They had a role to fill, different from that of other Jews, and at certain times more visible, and so were given appropriate respect for that role and what they represented. And so the old rabbi got out of the way for them, and even kissed their hands. But he was a dignified old sage and was in turn respected for who he was. Each had his own function, and neither's role took away from the importance or centrality of the other.

Closely watching all these goings-on with my prayer book in hand, I realized that the same principle applies to men and women in our beautiful Jewish tradition. Men and women are different, and therefore there are corresponding differences in the ways that will best help each gender develop a deeper connection with God and a more elevated, meaningful life. But different does not imply better or worse. Just like the *kohanim* are no better than non-*kohanim*, but sometimes fulfill different functions, men and women are not better or worse than each other but sometimes fulfill different functions.

This fundamental idea — that the Jewish tradition respects, values, and admires women as much as men — is not only lost to most Jewish women today, but also seems to be contradicted by the different roles each gender takes on. Many women thus feel estranged from their religious and cultural heritage, leading to disastrous consequences only a generation or two down the line.

The original *Jewish Matters* has already received wide acclaim in Jewish newspapers and magazines around the world. Its content and format fill an important niche — user-friendly, inspiring, and informative. No wonder institutions and individuals of various Jewish backgrounds have not only bought it for themselves, but have also given it to friends and colleagues in the hope of igniting a dormant Jewish spark.

I am therefore so pleased that the editors have put together *Jewish Women Speak*, a fitting sequel to the first in their series. They have asked some of the most knowledgeable and articulate female Jewish writers, teachers, and *rebbetzins* in the English-speaking world to share of their wisdom. This little volume will help us all gain a deeper understanding of the beauty of our tradition and the greatness of the Jewish woman. It is an essential enterprise and a wonderful and inspiring collection. May there be many more!

Barbara Stark
5760/2000

Introduction

We live in wonderful but complicated times. The technological and Web revolution is making things possible today that were unforeseen even ten years ago, and yet there are more and more poor around the world not getting a piece of the pie. There is much hope for peace in the Middle East, and yet the bumps along the way include risks that remind us that nothing is for certain. Women are achieving amazing levels of freedom, power, and economic independence, and yet statistics show frightening levels of frustration, depression, loneliness, and divorce. Across the spectrum of religious observance, age, and education, Jews are showing renewed interest in and commitment to their heritage, and yet over half of young Jews are marrying out of their religion.

Jewish women are particularly torn. Educated, independent, and successful, we are grateful for the unprecedented equality women have gained this century and unwilling to go back in time. True, we feel strongly about being Jewish, and our hearts have a special place for the Jewish tradition. But the status that classic Judaism seems to afford women prevents us from feeling any true closeness to our heritage. While we can choose to ignore the parts we don't like, in the end, how much warmth and admiration can we have for a tradition that doesn't respect us? It seems that Jewish women are forced to choose which will be their primary identification, feminism or Judaism. It is a terrible choice to have to make. No wonder so many young Jewish women are directly and indirectly marrying and assimilating out of Jewish history.

But it doesn't have to be this way. If we delve into our tradition with thought and openness, we will find — as more and more women are finding — something truly amazing. The same tradition that taught the world that all humans are brothers and sisters created in the image of God, the same tradition that teaches that one's animals are to be fed before oneself, the same tradition that gave the world its ideal of universal peace and brotherhood — that same tradition views and treats women as complete equals deserving of the same respect men deserve.

This may not be obvious at first to the outside observer, but, as in most areas of life, first glances are deceiving. In reality, Jewish women can feel completely connected to their womanhood without ignoring any of their tradition and completely connected to their tradition without denying any of their womanhood. If we delve into our tradition with sincerity and curiosity, we will discover the great honor and incredible gift of being a Jewish woman.

Speaking about...
Spiritual Matters

"I think modern Jewish women should realize they have a place in world history. We are an essential, integral part of Jewish life and tradition. Judaism has given the world its great values — from belief in God to caring for one another. Whenever I light candles on Friday afternoons, I remember that the Jewish people, and especially the women, bring light into what is still a very dark, sad world. I put myself in touch with the Jewish people: past, present, and future." — Debbie, 23

"You start with something simple and meaningful. Slowly, bit by bit, this whole tradition becomes your own; you find yourself in it. You find yourself in it as a person, a Jew, a woman, a wife, and a mother. Even if you begin without much belief, after a while just by practicing on a day-to-day basis you develop an understanding. You need no convincing. The whole thing just makes such good sense." — Heather, 28

"Many people go through their lives believing that they are not really important. Movie stars are important. Politicians are important. Little old me, I'm not really important in the big scheme of things. This belief can lead to feelings of inadequacy, hopelessness, and depression. Judaism teaches that we are important. Each one of us is part of something. If you are here, you have a job to do. No matter how old you are or what your life situation is, you are important." — Ruth, 63

"The Jewish tradition has survived the test of time. It has provided stability and happiness to millions of people over thousands of years. In America it seems the whole moral order changes every twenty years. How do you know what is really right?" — Melanie, 22

Rebbetzin Tzipora Heller

The Jewish Woman's Path to Spirituality

W omen's roles in Judaism during the last twenty years have been largely viewed in negative terms: why *can't* a woman do such-and-such? Rarely has the focus been on what the spiritual life of Jewish women traditionally has consisted of, as if Jewish women for the last three thousand years have done nothing except diaper babies while their husbands rose to spiritual heights through prayer and Torah study.

In fact, no one truly knowledgeable of Jewish history could contend that Judaism throughout the ages has produced more saintly men than saintly women. While it may be true that the former have had more publicity, for a religion that maintains that the world is sustained by the merit of thirty-six hidden saints, fame is obviously no measure of spiritual attainment.

One of the basic spiritual practices of Jewish women for the last 3,650 years has been prayer. Indeed, the Talmud tells us that because God loves the prayers of the righteous, the matriarchs were created barren so that they would have to pray for children.

It is of great significance that the laws of prayer were developed by the Sages of the Talmud by using a woman, Hannah, as the role model. Her prayers, as narrated in the first chapters of the book of Samuel, contain within them the very core of Jewish prayer structure. Specifically, the following practices stem from her methods:

1. She prayed silently. The central prayer of every Jewish prayer service, the standing prayer known as the Amidah, is thus recited under one's breath. Although our lips move, no sounds are heard. This signifies the reality that God hears our thoughts and does not need them verbalized. The need to use speech in prayer at all is related to the fact that we are affected by the sound of our words, and they help delineate our thoughts for us. Speech also makes the interaction all the more real to us. Hence our prayers are verbal, but in deference to Hannah's insights into prayer's true nature, they are silent.

2. The text explicitly makes note of Hannah's prayer as being an outpouring of her heart. It is all too easy for prayer to be said by rote, with the focus on completing the service rather than its genuine essence. Hannah taught us that prayer must be a connection between oneself and God. This means prayer must be more than just saying the words; you have to mean it.

Prayer Today

Most major interpretations of Jewish law teach that women are obligated to pray the morning and afternoon prayers (men are obligated in these and an additional evening prayer). All sources agree that women are obligated to fulfill the commandment of doing the "service of the heart" by praying every day in some way. The minimal fulfillment of this would be a short prayer of one's own composition that includes praise of God, a request, and thanks.

The historical reality is that Jewish women throughout the ages have additionally undertaken the recital of the book of Psalms as their specific avenue of prayer.

These prayers are particularly suited to women's lifestyles because one can interrupt their recitation at the end of every line (when a neighbor needs a sympathetic ear, when lunch break is cut short, when the baby cries). The standard prayer service should not be interrupted except at certain points, and it is forbidden to interrupt the silent standing prayer at all.

To this day, women can be seen fervently reciting psalms at the Western Wall in Jerusalem at every hour of the day and night. The seriousness and power of their prayer is evident even to the casual observer. And in religious communities throughout the world, women will invariably respond to news of illness or other impending catastrophes by getting together to recite these songs of praise and supplication. In this age of modern women earnestly seeking to find their spiritual path in Judaism, one must marvel that for many this ancient and powerful practice of saying psalms goes largely ignored. Its power to work wonders is attested to by the old Yiddish saying, "Don't rely on miracles. Say psalms!"

Home Prayer

Jewish women most often pray at home for several reasons. The first is that, unlike men, they are not obligated to pray at set times or in a group of ten. This gives women the freedom to pray according to their convenience (although the morning prayer must be said sometime before noon and the afternoon prayer before sunset), in solitude, and at their own pace, which many women find more conducive to concentration and devotion. In fact, a common complaint one hears from men who begin praying more often in synagogue is the difficulty of keeping up with the quorum while at the same time concentrating on the words they are saying.

Praying at home is also more convenient for mothers who choose to stay home with their small children, which is why the ladies' sections of Orthodox synagogues generally are occupied by older women. This, however, should not be misunderstood to mean that younger women do not pray.

One of my students told me of a pivotal point in her life. A very spiritual young woman who spent long periods each day in prayer and meditation, she was afraid that having a family would leave her no room for her inner life. Then she was invited to Sabbath dinner at the home of a family with many children. During the meal, she asked the mother if she ever prayed and was surprised to hear that she did — twice every day. Seeing her astonishment, the mother added, "That's nothing. I have a cousin who has even more kids, and she prays, with concentration, three times a day."

Another reason most women prefer to pray privately relates to the holiness of the Jewish home. Some people view the home as a place to rest between the more important places in which we spend our time, like the office or the theater. Judaism sees the home as a place of warmth and holiness, and the most central facets of our tradition (Shabbat, mikveh, and keeping kosher) are all home-based. Praying there both partakes of this sanctity and adds to it. The home is in no way less important than the synagogue — they are both sanctuaries of God.

In times and places where a large proportion of Jewish women did go to synagogue, the women's galleries are grand and spacious. (Witness the magnificent old synagogues of Calcutta and Amsterdam.) In places and periods where they usually did not, the women's sections were correspondingly paid little attention; some old synagogues have none at all. A common phenomenon today is for tourists to go to synagogues in Jerusalem's Meah Shearim neighborhood and complain that the women's section is cramped and claustrophobic, as if women were being purposely discouraged from coming to pray. In fact, the builders of these synagogues a half-century or century ago never expected that these women would be coming to visit, or even that sociological changes would cause more local women to attend services. The newest chassidic synagogue in that area, the Boyaner shul, boasts a spacious, airy, and well-lit women's gallery.

The Spirit of Separation

Prayer is a serious spiritual practice designed to connect us with our Creator; it is not a spectator sport. That some women complain of their lack of a view in synagogue, rather than their lack of prayerful concentration or communion with God, reveals a total misconception about why anyone should be there in the first place. Once we understand that the purpose of prayer is to develop a connection with God, we gain a new perspective on why men and women sit separately in the synagogue.

The ideal state for a person to be in when praying is to envision him or herself as part of the community (emphasizing our connection to and concern for others) yet simultaneously alone with God. In order to create an environment conducive to this, distractions are limited. Praying outdoors, for example, is not as desirable in Jewish law as praying indoors. In the synagogue, mirrors are forbidden, and pictures are considered a distraction (which is why there is no true synagogue art parallel to cathedral art). We are not to look out of the windows during prayer. If possible, one should pray facing a wall with one's eyes either closed or looking at a prayer book. Lack of visibility of the opposite sex at this time is part of the generalized effort to eliminate distractions.

Human nature being what it is, in synagogues that

have mixed seating or very low partitions, the ambience of "going to synagogue" is sometimes more like a singles' mixer than a spiritual encounter. Partitions were set up almost three thousand years ago to help both men and women accomplish what they came to do: develop a connection with God.

The Root of the Difference

Judaism maintains that God created men and women inherently and nonnegotiably different in specific areas. This contrasts fundamentally with views that insist that, except for the obvious physical distinctions, there are no significant inherent divergences between men and women.

In Jewish thought, however, not only do women differ from men physically, emotionally, intellectually, and spiritually, but these differences are beneficial for both sexes — "difference" needs not imply difference in value. We often are inclined to appraise differences in terms of relative worth — better or worse, prettier or uglier. Judaism maintains that a dog is not worse than a cat because it is less agile, more easily excitable, and takes longer to housebreak. Nor is a cat worse than a dog because it is less playful or more aloof. There is an unswerving belief in the integrity of pluralism.

One of these differences is in the way men and women commune with their Creator. Our tradition tells us clearly that women need more flexibility in their spiritual paths than men do. The absence of externally imposed structure does not mean that doing anything with one's time is as good as doing anything else. Women are not given more freedom because less is expected of them; on the contrary, Judaism assumes that women are capable of finding equally growth-producing outlets for their energies on their own. A woman who stays in bed happily reading *People* magazine while her husband is praying in the synagogue is totally missing the boat; worse than that, she is failing to live up to God's expectations of her.

The corollary to the belief that a woman does not need such obligations as communal prayer (or for that matter, tefillin) is not that she can instead do anything she pleases and still reap the same spiritual rewards as a man. It is rather that she possesses the potential to make the best choices as to how she can optimally use her time and is accordingly given the opportunity to do so. The rest is up to her.

Women have the choice to attend or not attend synagogue. If a woman finds that synagogue prayer answers her spiritual needs, she should go. If not, she should pray at home. Not praying is not an option — women's prayers are just as needed and important as men's. Since women are not obligated to pray in a minyan (quorum), they are not counted as part of one even when they attend (Jewish practice is based on obligations, not rights). This is not an insult to women — our prayers are heard just as well individually. Imagine if women were told they had to pray together three times a day in order for their prayers to be heard like those of a lone man at home!

The road to true equality between the sexes lies in establishing true mutual respect and appreciation. The cornerstone of the entire Jewish view of male and female roles, then, is the premise that gender differences are real and good. They were created with great wisdom and are meant to be acknowledged and used creatively and constructively as both genders move forward on their parallel — but different — spiritual paths.

REBBETZIN TZIPORA HELLER is an internationally known lecturer and scholar of Jewish studies. Since 1980 she has been a full-time faculty member of Neve

Yerushalayim College in Jerusalem, where her areas of expertise include textual analysis of biblical literature, Jewish philosophy, the role of women in Judaism, and analyses of the lives of women in the Bible and Prophets. She has been a visiting lecturer at Hebrew University, the Weizmann Institute, the University of Haifa, and many other institutions in and out of Israel and is the author of *More Precious than Pearls: Qualities of the Ideal Woman* (Feldheim Publishers) and the soon-to-be- published *Our Bodies, Our Souls.*

Rebbetzin Denah Weinberg

Shabbat Candles:
The Lights of the Soul

L ook around. The world is a dark place. People are wandering, roaming the world, searching for meaning. They are trying out this philosophy, that religion. People are groping. Where are the answers? Where is the light?

Light was created on the first day, and the Torah says, "It was good."

It is a woman's mitzvah to light the Shabbat candles. It is a woman's privilege to bring good into the world through light. How can those two little flickering candles on my table light up the big, dark world?

The Shabbat candles usher in the holy day of Shabbat. Thus those little candle lights direct us to a much greater light, the light of Shabbat.

Shabbat Is a Big, Big Light

The light at the end of the tunnel is bright — it breaks the darkness. Shabbat also breaks the darkness. It is not just a day when we stop working. Shabbat is the Day of the Candles, the Day of Light, the day when we clearly see our purpose in this world. Shabbat is the day on which we see we have a soul.

The soul itself is called a candle — "the candle of God." It is the light of the world. It infuses spirituality into the body and into all materialism. Without this spirituality, the world would be in a state of darkness. It is the soul that connects human beings to God. Similarly, Shabbat is the soul of the week. Without Shabbat, the world is a body without a soul. When women light candles, we welcome that extra light into the world.

Do you know that Shabbat also gives us an extra soul? During the rest of the week, one soul is powerful enough to receive the available holiness. But we need two souls to handle all the extra holiness that enters the world on Shabbat.

It is all too easy to ignore the extra soul and the extra spirituality that is available every Shabbat and to spend the day just eating and sleeping. We need to ask ourselves, "Is this the most efficient use of an extra soul?"

I once heard it said that it's much easier to overcome internal conflicts on Shabbat than all week, because during the week the odds are one against one — one body versus one soul. But on Shabbat, it is two against one — two souls versus one body. On Shabbat we have a real chance to be more in control.

Candles are lit at romantic dinners, aren't they? What makes a dimly lit room romantic? It's the candles — they draw people together on a soul level. It goes beyond eating a meal together — that's mundane, that's physical. Rather, it's about two humans connecting on a deep, spiritual level. That's exciting. That's romantic! The candles do it.

This, too, is Shabbat. The candles draw us to each other, and they draw us to God. Our soul is drawn to Him and vice versa. Shabbat is a love song. It is romance. It is a date between God and us. (Remember, on Shabbat, don't concentrate on your food — concentrate on your date!)

We women are the ones who "ignite" this romance with God. This is what Shabbat candle lighting is all about.

So let's not run out of the shower or from last-minute preparations to light the Shabbat candles. Let's give our mitzvah some thought and put it into its proper spiritual dimension. Do you feel the light on Shabbat? Do you feel your soul light up?

Our tradition gives us guidelines to experience the spiritual dimension of candle lighting. Buy beautiful candlesticks; make sure they and the tray they rest on are polished to emphasize the importance of this mitzvah. Lighting with olive oil is highly regarded because of the intense light it produces. Be dressed in beautiful clothes at candle lighting time and, of course, be on time. Prepare, think, and be focused on this great experience.

Our tradition also tells us something remarkable. To help her children fulfill their potential, a woman should feel tremendous happiness when lighting her Shabbat candles. What won't parents do to have good children? They pay high tuition for the best schools; give them extracurricular activities, hobbies, and vacations to stimulate their minds and strengthen their bodies; feed them good, healthy meals; and buy them fine clothes. Yet Jewish sources tell us that one of the most important things we can do for our children is to be careful and happy when lighting Shabbat candles. This is our investment for meriting good, wise, and spiritually fulfilled Jewish children.

Shabbat candles also create peace in the home. How? People enjoy the Shabbat food more with the added light. And there is something deeper. Candles connect people on a spiritual level. Souls don't fight. Bodies fight. Candlelight evokes a soul connection between people, which creates real peace in the home.

Shabbat reminds us that there was a creation and a Creator. Just as Shabbat comes after six days of work, our ultimate connection to God comes in the World to Come — after years and years of work! This is clarity. This brings sanity.

Human beings ask, "What are we living for?" The Light of Shabbat answers, "For an eternity of light, warmth, and closeness to our loving God."

Shabbat is the goal of the week, not merely a rest stop to prepare for the coming week. In truth, we work all week long for this day of pleasure. There is even a tradition to count the days in anticipation of Shabbat. "We're getting there.... We're almost there.... We're here!" It's like a bride counting the days to her wedding — not because the wedding will mark the end of her preparations, but because it is the goal.

Shabbat is our goal, our destination. On Shabbat, all difficulties of the previous week change into a new reality. On Shabbat, all pain changes into beautiful, new challenges.

May we light the candles joyfully, carefully, and happily until the world is lit completely with the lights of Shabbat.

REBBETZIN DENAH WEINBERG is dean and director of E.Y.A.H.T., Aish HaTorah's College for Women in Jerusalem. Born and educated in Far Rockaway, New York, she has lived in Israel for many years. She has been a world-renowned lecturer for over three decades and has helped thousands of women to grow and maximize their potential to greatness. She is particularly well known for teaching Jewish women how to get the most out of Shabbat, and this essay is adapted from one of her most famous lectures on the subject.

Dr. Lisa Aiken

My Secret Romance

I must confess that I have been having a secret romance for most of my adult life. It all started innocently enough when I was in graduate school studying for my doctorate in clinical psychology. I decided we should try to meet for an hour a day, wherever we could rendezvous. Sometimes we met in public places, such as classes or even in the synagogue. Often we met in libraries. At least once a week we stole time together while riding the bus or subway to school. Before I knew it, I had become addicted to the thrill of these encounters.

Who was my lover? It was none other than God Himself communicating with me through my study of Torah.

My Lover's Gift

One of the beauties of the Torah is that everything a person could want to know is in there if we only try to drink from its unending fountains of wisdom. It teaches us about ourselves. It explains why we were put into this world, how we can live a meaningful life, develop our spirituality, and become better people. As a psychologist, I found myself especially drawn to the Torah's revelations about how people can find the right balance between giving and taking, be self-disciplined yet full of feeling. It gives us guidelines for how best to relate to others, how we can (and should) learn to control our impulses and our anger, how we can fix our negative character traits and highlight our positive ones. In short, the Torah teaches us how we can truly actualize ourselves in ways that modern psychology has yet to show us.

Many modern views of our self-worth and how we should live seem so trivializing. They are full of shallow ideas such as "find pleasure," "do what makes you feel good," "get in touch with your anger," and "get rid of your guilt." In contrast, Torah is rich and deep. Its values are real and enduring. It saddens me that more people don't know what it has to offer.

The Torah teaches us that we are not glorified animals — unless, of course, we choose to live that way. We are potentially great because God chose to create each and every one of us. He took the effort to put us in this world at a specific time, in a specific place, in order to do a specific job that no one else can do. How can we not have strong self-esteem when we realize that the Creator of the universe has entrusted us with an important job and is waiting for us to complete it? How can we not feel loved as our study of Torah attunes us to God's warm embrace, especially during times of crisis and challenge?

True, but...

While some women approach the idea of Torah study with excitement, others feel intimidated. They are interested in being more educated about Judaism, but they feel they are too old to start, that it would be humiliating to learn with people who know more than they do, or that Torah study is only for men.

Our tradition tells a story about Rabbi Akiva, who lived about nineteen hundred years ago. He was an illiterate shepherd until he was forty years old. One day he saw a channel that flowing water had cut into a rock. He reasoned that if with persistence water could cut something as hard as rock, he could certainly etch Torah into his untutored mind were he only to apply himself.

With his wife's support, he left home to study Torah and started his Jewish education by learning the Hebrew alphabet like the three-year-olds of the time. When he returned from the study hall much later, he had become one of the greatest Torah scholars who ever lived. (He also publicly told his twenty-four thousand students that everything he had learned, and everything they had learned, they owed to his wife's constant support.) The point is that Jewish education can add enormously to life, in any situation, at any age.

In our generation, Jewish women have risen to the highest levels of secular knowledge and career advancement. We owe it to ourselves to take advantage of the unprecedented opportunities presently available to be Jewishly educated as well. History has shown that where there is no Jewish learning there are soon no Jews. Jewish women need to study Torah because it provides the knowledge and inspiration necessary to be caring and committed Jews. Furthermore, we live in a material world where people often can't see past the allures and pleasures of the moment. If we are interested in hearing God communicate to us, there is no better way to sensitize our antennae than to study how God reveals Himself in our world — through the Torah.

Where to Start

Many women who have not had an intensive Jewish education are unsure about where they should begin learning about Judaism. Here are a few suggestions:

1. *Find a mentor and ask for recommendations.*

While one can learn a great deal from books and audiocassettes, knowing what to focus on and what to avoid can be important. Just because something is in print doesn't mean it is well written, appropriate for you, or even true. Think about what interests you, then find someone knowledgeable (and sincere) to direct you to classes, books, or tapes that would be appropriate for you given your background and interests.

2. *Get connected.*

Almost every city has adult classes available on a variety of Jewish topics. Your local Jewish bookstore is usually an excellent place to find out what is offered in your area. Alternatively, the Partners-in-Torah toll free phone number (1-800-STUDY-4-2) will help you find out about options available in your locale.

If you don't live or work near available classes, you can sign up with Jewish education Web sites. These send out daily or weekly Torah discussions about any topic that interests you, such as the Bible and its commentaries, the Jewish lifecycle, holidays, prayer, Jewish philosophy, Jewish history, Jewish law (including how to celebrate Shabbat and keep a kosher home), the oral law, mysticism, and perspectives on dating, marriage, raising children, and character improvement. Some popular Web sites to start with are aish.com, www.chabadonline.com, www.ohr.org.il, and www.torah.org.

3. *Get a study partner.*

The traditional Jewish study system is based on *chavruta*s, or study partners, who progress together through texts. Learning this way is both fun and effective. You might want to start with someone more knowledgeable than you to get the ball rolling smoothly. Don't try to take on too much — an hour or two once a week on a regular basis is already a major step in becoming Jewishly educated. If you don't know anyone to study with, the nonprofit organization called

Partners-in-Torah will find someone for you to study with, either in person or by phone, wherever you are in North America (free long-distance phone cards provided; call them at 1-800-STUDY-4-2).

Once you start on your journey, you can expect that some areas will interest you more than others. It's nice to study at least one area that excites you, where every encounter adds to your knowledge and fuels you to learn more. You may also find that as time passes your tastes change. I was once a bookstore junkie, taking most of my savings and buying sets of English commentaries on the Torah. While I gained enormously from my reading, I soon realized that I needed a real person to teach me and answer my questions. My next step was to find classes, tutors, and friends to study with. In this way I was able to develop the skills necessary to analyze texts on my own. Later on, I discovered the amazing world of audiocassette Torah study. I realized how much I had studied at home and in my car during the prior two years when I had to pack the more than six hundred tapes I had bought and listened to!

Growing Together

Judaism teaches that life is about developing a relationship with God. This relationship is expressed directly — for example, in our prayers — and also in the way we relate to others and to the physical world around us. As we mature, the depth of this relationship should also mature. As our knowledge and understanding of life grows throughout our lives, so our knowledge and understanding of Judaism should also grow. In this way, we can connect to the Divine more and more closely and develop a full appreciation of life and its opportunities. No matter what our backgrounds, no matter what our ages, it is never too late to start learning about our religion, our history, our souls, and ourselves. The path is not as difficult as we may think, and the reward is heavenly.

DR. LISA AIKEN is a practicing psychologist in New York City and Great Neck, Long Island. From 1982–89, she was chief psychologist at Lennox Hill Hospital in New York City and a clinical assistant professor at New York Medical College. She has lectured for diverse Jewish groups and other organizations in over a hundred cities on four continents, has an extensive tape collection, and has appeared on radio and television. She is coauthor of *The Art of Jewish Prayer* with Rabbi Yitzchak Kirzner, *zt"l*, and wrote *To Be a Jewish Woman, Why Me, God?: A Jewish Guide for Coping with Suffering, Beyond Bashert: A Guide to Dating and Marriage Enrichment,* and *The Hidden Beauty of the Shema.*

Rebbetzin Holly Pavlov

The Woman's Holiday

A tiny sliver of the moon appears. Rosh Chodesh, the day of the new moon, has arrived, symbolizing the constant renewal of the world.

Rosh Chodesh is a day of happiness and rejoicing. It is celebrated by reciting special prayers, and many people eat a festive meal and/or dress up for the occasion. For the Jewish woman, Rosh Chodesh is even more — it is a holiday given exclusively to us, celebrated with extra joy and an abstention from unnecessary work. How did Jewish women earn this special holiday?

When the Jewish people stood at Mount Sinai, they were told that Moses would ascend the mountain for forty days to receive the Torah. They waited for his descent, but miscalculated. When the fortieth day arrived — according to their tally — and their leader had not returned, they became frightened.

Some men decided to create a substitute leader — an idol. They gathered gold with which to make it and demanded that their wives contribute their gold as well, but the women refused to participate. Instinctively, the women understood the depth of the tragic mistake their husbands were about to make. They declared, "We will not help you in order to make an abomination that has no power." The men refused to listen, gave their own gold, and grabbed the earrings from their wives' ears.

They threw the jewelry into the fire, from which a golden calf emerged.

In the aftermath, the men were punished for their actions, while the women were rewarded for their loyalty and trust in God. Their reward was an extra holiday — Rosh Chodesh. Although it is clear that the women deserved to be rewarded, how is Rosh Chodesh in particular fitting for what occurred? What is the connection between the women's actions and the holiday they were given?

To answer our question, let us look at an interesting conversation recorded in the Talmud. We are taught that on the fourth day of Creation God created two great lights, the sun and the moon. Originally, both were equal in size. The moon complained, saying, "Is it possible for two kings to wear one crown?" God answered the moon, "Go, then, and make yourself smaller." And thus it is that the moon is smaller than the sun.

At a deeper level, this account can help us understand the relationship between human beings and God. In a sense, there is a deep contradiction within us. Although it appears that we are the rulers of the world — having intellect, understanding, and abilities far beyond any animal — in reality we are only faint images of God's true essence. Everything we have and are comes from Above. Just as the moon brings none of its own light into the world, but merely reflects that of the sun, so too we have no real capabilities of our own. All that we can accomplish we owe to the strength, intellect, and talents we receive from God.

The moon understood that it is impossible for two kings to wear the same crown. One must submit to the other. So too, human beings must realize that God is the one and only Ruler of the universe.

Those who worshiped the golden calf stumbled.

When events didn't proceed exactly the way they expected them to, they attempted to fashion a more accessible god, one that would meet the fictitious needs of the moment. They wanted a god they could fully understand and control, one who wasn't really greater than them at all. Essentially, when it became inconvenient, they no longer wished to be subservient to God.

By refusing to participate in the creation of the golden calf, Jewish women displayed their profound understanding that the creation and worship of an idol was a violation of what God wanted of them. Their willingness to subjugate themselves to their true King — to be "small" in deference to God's greatness — brought them the reward of a holiday that commemorates this truth, by celebrating the moon's renewed cycle.

The women at Sinai understood that along with free will comes the responsibility to choose well. In aligning themselves with God, they became a reflection of Him. As the moon waxes and wanes in a monthly cycle, consistently demonstrating that it can bring more or less light into the world, we too have the choice of bringing more or less light into the world. May we continue to follow in the footsteps of the righteous women of Israel, always reflecting the will of God — and lighting up the world.

REBBETZIN HOLLY PAVLOV is a veteran Jewish educator and administrator with over thirty years of experience. In order to meet the unique needs of today's Jewish woman, Rebbetzin Pavlov and a group of dedicated colleagues opened She'arim College of Jewish Studies for Women in the fall of 1994. Rebbetzin Pavlov is a sought-after expert in teaching textual skills, as well as an internationally noted speaker on Midrash, Jewish philosophy, and ethics. Her wholehearted and sincere dedication to her students creates the unique, warm atmosphere for which She'arim is famous. Rebbetzin Pavlov is the author of *Mirrors of Our Lives: Reflections of*

Women in Tanach. Her book emphasizes the lessons we can learn from the personalities, life experiences, and struggles of our matriarchs.

Speaking about...
Body and Soul

"The casual way that relationships were formed and evolved on campus simply went against my grain. Is this what life is about? Look at the results: most marriages end in divorce and even those that don't are often unhappy or boring. I wanted a nice relationship with my husband. And I knew where to find it — in our tradition." — Lisa, 27

"When I took counseling courses in graduate school, I was taught that after a few years of marriage a couple may lose interest in each other, and the best advice we were given to help was to encourage periodic abstention." — Denise, 38

I can look beautiful, but why do I have to show everything? Why are thirteen-year-old girls today wearing tank tops? Why do their parents let them?" — Frances, 28

"The mikveh cycle of separations and reunions restores our passion and safeguards a wonderful intimate life. It is mind-boggling to think that this wonderful Torah has known who I am as a woman for thousands of years." — Sharon, 33

"When I looked into it, it became clear to me that the Jewish way of life is simply the most ethical, rational, and psychologically sane way to live. — Claire, 36

Chana Kalsmith

A Vision of Beauty

E very good restaurant knows the importance of
garnishing a dish to make it more appetizing,
but you will rarely find a dog owner adding a
sprig of parsley to his dog's Puppy Chow to get his dog
to eat. Nor will you see a goat stop on the mountainside
and gaze out at the world, awed by its splendor. You
never have to speak to your cat about losing some
weight in order to meet the right match. Only human
beings seem to appreciate aesthetics.

Like everything in the world, our Creator gave us
this appreciation for a purpose. In order to understand
this purpose, we will look into the Torah and explore
the Jewish view of beauty.

> God caused every kind of tree to grow from the
> ground, attractive to the sight and good for
> food....
>
> (Genesis 2:9)

The famous commentator Rabbi Samson Raphael
Hirsch asks why this verse mentions "attractive to the
sight" before "good for food." He explains that "satisfying man's appreciation of beauty comes before gratify-
ing his sense of taste and fulfilling his need for
nourishment. This verse justifies and sanctifies our involvement with aesthetics. In fact, the human apprecia-

tion of beauty may indicate the higher place intended for man in the scheme of creation. The abundance of beautiful creations on earth and the fact that, as far as we know it, man is the only creature endowed with a sense for enjoying beauty, indicate that the Creator deemed a sense of aesthetics fundamental for man's spiritual and moral calling.

"Indeed, the beautiful sights scattered throughout creation, along with man's capacity for deriving pleasure from them, are the principal means for protecting man from becoming completely debased. The pleasure man derives from the beauty in nature and from the beautiful forms with which God fashioned the world, in particular the plant world, is a bridge to deriving pleasure from moral beauty.

"The sensitivity to harmony and order in the physical world is related to the sensitivity to harmony and order in the sphere of ethics. In an environment where no consideration is given to harmony and beauty, man can easily become wild. The Hebrew word for evil, ra, is related to the word ra'a, which literally means 'that which is broken.' Evil appears to us as something broken, a disturbance in harmony in which the whole is no longer ruled by one uniform thought."

Rabbi Hirsch is telling us that beauty is order and that an appreciation of physical order will lead to an appreciation of moral order.

How does this work? By teaching us that order is pleasurable. After all, physical beauty is essentially a combination of symmetry, harmony, and order. When the grass is green and the sky is blue and the clouds are white, it's a beautiful day. There are people in the world that everyone would agree are beautiful to look at — they have symmetrical features, their complexion and hair coloring present a harmonious image. This physical beauty exists to help us appreciate order on a moral level.

This may be one of the reasons that humans, as opposed to animals, were created with an appreciation of beauty. As human beings, we are in charge of the morality of the world. We can help others and act justly or (God forbid) create holocausts. The human appreciation of beauty exists in order to help us fulfill our higher purpose. We must recognize that there is an order to the world and that order is pleasing on all levels, physical as well as moral.

Now that we understand why aesthetics exist, we must know why some things are more beautiful than others. Why did God create a world with such varied levels of beauty?

The Beauty Deception

The Jewish tradition teaches us that the Garden of Eden was a world of truth where outward appearance naturally reflected inner being. Whatever looked beautiful was in fact good. A beautiful apple was healthy to eat, while a poisonous mushroom looked foreboding. Beauty indicated goodness. After Adam and Eve ate from the tree of knowledge, beauty and goodness were separated. Everything beautiful was not necessarily good, and everything good was not necessarily beautiful. This deception exists until today.

I learned this lesson well when visiting Yad VaShem, the Israeli national Holocaust museum, in Jerusalem about ten years ago. There was a painting in the exhibit that depicted a beautiful sunrise over a landscape of mountains. As I approached to have a better look, I saw that the mountains were in fact corpses piled on top of one another and that the sunrise was actually a fire from the crematorium. The image was horrible, violent, and tragic. The painter had captured the horror of affluent, cultured Germany with its evil core. Superficial glances are certainly deceiving.

Thousands of years after the Garden of Eden, we still have the God-given gift of appreciating aesthetics and naturally want things that look beautiful to be good. We expect a country that is cultured to be humane. Likewise, a person who is beautiful we hope will act beautifully. Yet today, what is beautiful physically and what is good morally can be quite different. We must look beyond surface beauty to ensure that what is shown to be beautiful is, in fact, good. We need to look into our heritage to relearn what is meant by true beauty. Let's explore this idea by focusing on beauty as it relates to people.

Beauty Should Reflect Beauty

What is true beauty? Most often, when the Torah mentions a beautiful person, it is referring to a person whose outer appearance reflects their inner soul. For example, we are taught about the beauty of our matriarch Sarah. According to our tradition, other women looked like monkeys compared to Sarah. The Talmud says that Sarah was as beautiful at the age of twenty as a seven-year-old child. Yet isn't twenty closer to the ideal age of beauty than seven? What is it about a child that is more beautiful than a young woman?

The explanation is simple. The beauty of children is the beauty of purity of spirit; they act the way they feel without being influenced by insincerity. There are no put-ons or pretending. As Rabbi Hirsch states, "The secret of beauty does not lie in superficial cosmetics but can be acquired only from within.... Only a beautiful, pure spirit, inspired by the spirit of God, can produce a physical image of angelic beauty." Sarah's beauty was one of complete synchronization between external and internal, between body and soul. This kind of beauty does not fade with age, pregnancy, or weight gain. It is a beauty that is cultivated inwardly and shines forth.

Judaism teaches that we all have precious souls and that externals should reflect this inner beauty. For example, both men and women are encouraged to maintain an attractive, dignified appearance. Jewish law forbids a Torah scholar to wear ripped or stained clothing. Our priests, the *kohanim*, could not perform the service in the Holy Temple in Jerusalem without the appropriate attire. We are not to become gluttonous or mistreat our bodies by overindulgence or self-mutilation. In essence, our bodies should be treated and dressed with respect, since they house what is most precious and beautiful — our souls.

I was once asked a very disturbing question while teaching about this concept. A student said to me, "Why should I dress like I'm dignified if I feel worthless inside?" The answer is that God created every person in the Divine image. We all have the beauty of this Divine image — the soul — inside us. Our external appearance should reflect its internal presence even if we don't always feel it.

This is true in mitzvot (commandments) as well. We are supposed to "beautify" the mitzvot. Most traditional homes have beautiful silver candlesticks for lighting Shabbat candles and a silver Kiddush cup to hold the wine over which we make a blessing on Shabbat. The Torah scroll itself is encased in fine cloth and laden with gold, silver, and precious jewels. The idea is that the mitzvah itself is spiritually beautiful and should be reflected that way in the physical world as well, in the same way that the body should reflect the beauty it holds.

The Challenge of Physical Beauty

Though it's true that we all have beautiful souls, some people were created objectively beautiful. Like intelligence, wealth, and strength, physical beauty is a gift. God creates different people with different gifts, and each person has the exact gift needed to reach his or her potential.

Every gift is also a challenge. For people with the gift of physical beauty, the challenge may be to avoid getting "hung up" on their beauty. Often they must overcome their beauty in order to develop their inner characters. Since they are given attention for their looks, there is less motivation to develop their character. For these people, the challenge is consistency. The physical beauty they were given on the outside should reflect the spiritual beauty they need to develop on the inside.

What about those people created without objective physical beauty? I first came to understand this situation while sitting in a class taught by Rebbetzin Tzipora Heller. She spoke about a fascinating story from the Talmud, in tractate *Ta'anit* (7a). The Talmud tells the story of Rabbi Yehoshua the son of Chananiah and the daughter of the Roman Emperor.

Rabbi Yehoshua was known for his great wisdom. He was also known to be unattractive. One day the daughter of the emperor asked him why God would place so much beautiful wisdom in such an ugly vessel. He replied, "Your father keeps his fine wine in cheap earthenware vessels."

"What else should he put it in?" she answered.

He told her that fine wine should be placed in gold and silver vessels. She went back to the palace and had the wine transferred into golden vessels. Soon after, it all spoiled. When her father asked her to explain what happened, she told him about her conversation with Rabbi Yehoshua. The emperor called the great rabbi in and asked him, "Why did you tell her to do that?" Rabbi Yehoshua explained that he was answering her question. "Just like wine is better preserved in ugly vessels, so too Torah is better preserved in me." The emperor said to the rabbi, "But there are beautiful people who are learned," and the rabbi replied, "If they were ugly, they would have learned more."

God is all-powerful and gives us exactly what we need. Every trait and physical attribute was given to us to help us reach our potential, from the parents we have to the way we look. Without objective physical beauty, people have extra encouragement to work on themselves internally and therefore may have a greater chance to reach their potential. The less-than-attractive body can therefore help preserve the soul better, as Rabbi Yehoshua taught. Furthermore, as we said above, true beauty is when a beautiful soul shines forth. Therefore, a physically unattractive person can become beautiful when their internal beauty shines forth through their physical features. (This explains how some people become more beautiful the more you get to know them.) And this kind of beauty doesn't fade with time.

Breaking the Beauty Myth

Now that we understand the Jewish view of aesthetics, we need to consider how modern Western society views beauty. A casual drive through any major metropolitan city exposes one to seemingly limitless messages about beauty. The beauty referred to, however, is only skin deep. Women on billboards look more like prowlers than people, ready to seduce whoever comes their way. Advertisements tell us how to be "beautiful." There are beauty products to stop the aging process, liposuction to get rid of excess fat, plastic surgery.... The list goes on.

Sadly, advertisements reflect the reality that most people don't realize what true beauty is — inner beauty reflected through the physical. They focus only on skin-deep beauty. Yet we all age, and our bodies sag and wrinkle. Focusing too much on external beauty in ourselves and others will not help us in the long term, since that beauty doesn't last. It is wiser to invest in what is inside so that as we age the beauty of our souls can shine forth from within. After all, our souls are eternally beautiful.

CHANA KALSMITH has lectured on women's issues in Judaism in Europe, Israel, and the United States, combining her knowledge of Judaism and her education in women's studies to offer unique insights into some of the most challenging and sensitive issues Jewish women face today. She is a regularly featured speaker at the Aish HaTorah New York Center and the Jewish Renaissance Center and has taught at the popular Discovery program. Receiving her master's degree in higher education from the University of Maryland at College Park and completing her graduate work at Georgetown University, her professional background includes being executive director of the Women's Information Network in Washington, D.C., a two-thousand-member organization for women who work in the public and private sector.

Dina Coopersmith

Beneath the Surface: A Deeper Look at Modesty

You may have heard of the concept before. In Hebrew, it is known as *tzniut*, which is commonly translated as "modesty." Many people think it means an overconcern with hemlines, sleeve lengths, and necklines. If we look more deeply, however, we may uncover a new understanding of this idea.

In virtually every culture, clothes are a basic requirement. Even in the hottest tropical climates, the inhabitants wear some minimal form of clothing. Nowhere, however, do animals instinctively cover up. Why is this? What is the connection between human beings and clothing that spans all ages and cultures?

The truth is, it wasn't always like this. Once, our tradition tells us, human beings didn't wear clothing at all. Initially, Adam and Eve roamed around the Garden of Eden *au naturel*.

> They were both naked, the man and his wife, and they were not ashamed.
>
> (Genesis 2:25)

Yet after eating the forbidden fruit, a change took place in their feelings about clothing (or the lack thereof):

> And their eyes were opened, and they knew they were naked, and they sewed fig leaves....
>
> (Genesis 3:7)

What caused this change of attitude? Why cover up all of a sudden? The answer is rooted in an understanding of what happened to Adam and Eve during this period.

Adam and Eve, living in Paradise, were not supposed to eat from the tree of knowledge of good and evil. Our tradition tells us that when they disobeyed and ate of it, the tendency to do evil was internalized within the human psyche. Previously, humans had an intellectual choice between good and evil, but evil was external — essentially a philosophical issue — not an inner pull like it is today.

Initially, therefore, body and soul were in consonance with each other. The body was essentially an expression of the soul. For instance, when the soul wanted to pray to God, the body rose early and prayed. The soul wanted to grow and strive, so the body ate healthy foods in order to provide the necessary energy for the demanding task.

Now, post-sin, a dichotomy exists, almost a schizophrenia. The soul wants to pray, but the body groans, turns over, and shuts off the alarm clock. The soul strives to perfect itself, and the body wants to eat chocolate cake and lie on the beach. The body is no longer in the service of the soul; it no longer runs to do its bidding. Not only is the body not a reflection of the soul, but now the two often work at cross-purposes.

What does all this have to do with clothing and modesty?

When Adam and Eve were roaming around the Garden of Eden with their bodies reflecting their souls, there was no need to cover up. Physicality was a pure, innocent expression of a person's spirituality, of God's image within a human being. However, once evil was integrated inside them, focusing on the body could now distract the observer from appreciating the person's essence and personality. It therefore became necessary to de-emphasize the physical in order to reemphasize the spiritual — to cover up the body in order to let the soul shine through. This would allow physicality to reach its full potential.

Modesty, Men, and the Mishkan

So why does it seem like modesty applies more to women than to men? Doesn't this disharmony between body and soul apply to both men and women equally?

Yes. Modesty does in fact apply to everyone:

> [God] tells you, man, what He requires of you: only to do justice, love kindness, and walk modestly [hatzne'a] with your God.
>
> (Micah 6:8)

> ...And with the modest ones lies wisdom.
>
> (Proverbs 11:2)

The concept of modesty emphasizes focusing on expression of one's inner self and avoiding the trap of superficiality in all areas, including speech, thought, and deed. In our history, the most heroic acts (like the binding of Isaac and Jacob's struggle with the angel) were done in private, with no fanfare or publicity — and thus represent the essence of modesty. This modest approach to life applies to both genders. Yet, for the specific issue of clothing, the ramifications are more serious for women, as they are also, interestingly enough, for Torah scholars and for the Mishkan, the portable Tabernacle that preceded the Holy Temple in Jerusalem:

> Torah scholars should be extra modest in clothes and in their behavior.
>
> *(Derech Eretz Zuta 7)*

> From the day the Tabernacle was built, God said, "Modesty is appropriate."
>
> *(Tanchuma, Bemidbar 3)*

What do women, Torah scholars, and the Mishkan have in common?

Torah scholars are human beings who are granted a degree of awe from the public due to their tremendous Torah knowledge. To the extent that they represent God's word on earth, they deserve extra respect. However, if we are taken in by external charisma, good looks, and public-speaking skills, and do not discern their internal holiness, we have missed the boat. Their unique inner essence is so vital that it necessitates special external protection — extra physical modesty.

Similarly, the Tabernacle represents the dwelling place of God on earth. Its vessels and structure were made of the finest materials, including gold, silver, and beautiful fabrics. If we were to see it as a mere building devoid of spiritual content, we would be missing the purpose for which the Tabernacle was built — connecting to God. All the vessels, therefore, required special coverings to de-emphasize the sparkling fancy exterior, in order to enable us to focus on the awesome spirituality below the surface.

Woman's Rich Inner World

Just as Torah scholars contain within them awesome wisdom and the Tabernacle vessels contained awesome spirituality, women, according to Judaism, share a special trait called *binah*, loosely translated as "deep understanding." In the Torah, women are exemplified as having a rich inner world, possessing unique powers of insight and perception beyond logic and external facade. Through their deep understanding, they have the power to influence those around them. If women are viewed externally, devoid of internal character and spirituality, they are stripped of their unique gift and strength. Therefore, regarding clothing, there is more of a focus on modesty for women than for men.

Furthermore, a special danger exists that women will be degraded when societal focus remains on the external. Cultures that "respect" women primarily for their physical characteristics are much more likely to degrade and take advantage of them.

In view of this risk (coupled with the strong tendency among males to notice the physical), women are encouraged to place extra emphasis on their real beauty — their inner strengths, their souls.

The Beauty Within

> All of the honor of the daughter of the King is within.
>
> (Psalms 45:14)

Of course, none of this implies that women shouldn't look beautiful. In fact, if the physical is not distracting and the internal holiness is realized, it is a mitzvah to be beautiful. Just as the Tabernacle was stunningly beautiful and Torah scholars are commanded to pay special attention to their physical appearances, so too a woman, a unique vessel for a rich and potent inner essence, is further enhanced by a beautiful exterior, one that is now infused with spiritual content.

And that's what the concept of *tzniut* is all about.

DINA COOPERSMITH is a teacher at Midreshet Rachel College of Jewish Studies for Women and at Machon Gold. She received her bachelor's degree in Tanach and education from Michlalah Jerusalem College for Women and her master's in Jewish studies from Touro College. She lives in Jerusalem with her husband and children. Several of the ideas in this article are adapted from a lecture of Rabbi Zev Leff, "The Concept of Modesty."

Gila Manolson

Touch

Imagine yourself at a checkout counter. You have never liked shopping at this store because of its less-than-wonderful service. Today is no exception — you have been waiting to pay for what seems like an eternity. Finally your turn comes. You hand the slow-moving cashier your money. Usually you have to pick up your change off the counter, but today the cashier places it in your hand, and for a brief moment you feel the warmth of his or her hand on yours. Outside, afterward, you sense something strange. For some reason, you're feeling more warmly toward this store than before.

Another scene: You have just finished dining at a restaurant. The service is exceedingly slow. Your waiter, David, finally brings the bill. "Hope you enjoyed your meal," he says with a smile and a parting pat on the shoulder. Watching him return to the kitchen, you suddenly feel a surge of generosity and leave a far bigger tip than you had intended. On your way out, you comment to the manager about how little waiters earn for working so hard. "It all depends," he replies. "Take this new guy, Dave. We don't know how he does it, but he pulls in at least thirty percent more in tips than anyone else."

In each of the above incidents, both based on true stories, you have fallen prey to one of the most subtle yet powerful forces in human relations: touch.

Notice, incidentally, that in neither case was the touch sensual or even affectionate. Still, it had an undeniable effect, opening up new feelings of warmth and receptivity. Even when not fueled by desire, touch can leave people feeling distinctly warmer and more connected to each other. Touch works like SuperGlue: take two people who aren't opposed to connecting to each other, and touch will make them feel closer. And, like SuperGlue, it must be handled very carefully, or it will end up sticking things together that would be better off not stuck.

Shomer Negiah

Touching another person (in Hebrew, *"negiah"*), as casually as it's regarded in many circles, is far more powerful than most of us appreciate. Traditional Judaism, always an astute observer of the human scene, stipulates that men and women who are not close relatives should exercise extreme caution and sensitivity in expressing affection for one another through touch. In short, Judaism says, "Unless you're close relatives or married to each other, don't."

Understandably, this strikes some people as extreme. But the truth is that for anyone who's serious about getting the most out of a relationship — and avoiding the pain of failed ones — being *shomer negiah* (literally "guarding" or "saving touch" for the right person) makes eminent sense. Here's why.

Touch is a powerful force in making people feel closer. And, like any force, it can be harnessed constructively or destructively. Touch can be used to comfort — or to manipulate. It can foster group friendship — or cult-like attachment. Touch can increase intimacy between two people who truly love each other. But it can also create illusory feelings of intimacy and make you feel close to a person even when you are not really so close after all, creating many serious problems.

The Cloud Descends

The first problem is with objectivity. Touch is powerful enough to blur reality to the point where it seems that the closeness you feel is real. Once this happens, that all-too-familiar rose-colored cloud descends, enveloping everything in warm and glowing feelings of intimacy. At this point, you can kiss much of your perspective on your partner and the relationship goodbye. Valuable time and emotions can be wasted on the wrong person, because you never developed an objective view of who your partner really is. Many marriages fail quickly because the match was wrong to begin with, but the couple had become too enraptured with each other to notice it. You certainly wouldn't choose a business partner with blinders on, so why be less careful when it comes to a serious relationship?

Sensitivity

Most people ultimately want one lifelong partner with whom they can feel, as much and as deeply as possible, the positive uniqueness and singularity that is called "specialness." Physical intimacy, with all the feelings it engenders, is central to a successful marriage, and Judaism wants it to be special. By limiting this intimacy to your true partner, it becomes even more so. Each time you are physically involved with someone prior to your husband or wife, your sensitivity is dulled. While time brings about some resensitization, this most precious, intimate, and personal part of you has been shared with others before, and it can no longer be as special.

Comparisons

With each relationship before marriage, you open the door wider to innumerable comparisons between your future spouse and a past boyfriend or girlfriend. Since it is nearly impossible that your spouse will measure up in all areas — and since human beings have a strong tendency to focus on what they don't have at any given time — such comparisons can't do you or your relationship any good.

A friend of mine was teaching about this concept when a man (whose wife I assume was not present) volunteered the following delightful comment: "I know what you mean. I've been married for two years and I really love my wife, but even in our most intimate moments, I can't help thinking of my previous girlfriend." Memories of previous relationships have an uncanny way of surfacing when you least want them to, even years after they occur.

Emotional Scars

Human relationships are central to our lives. When you succeed in a relationship, your positive feelings about life are strengthened. But every time you get hit over the head emotionally, feelings of negativity and futility develop. With each breakup, you pay a price — your optimism and ability to trust are diminished. Time does heal, but scars remain. Your natural defense mechanisms have closed up parts of you that may be difficult to reopen, and the subconscious guards and blocks you've developed can profoundly interfere with the quality and depth of your future lifelong relationship. The best way to avoid getting hurt is to avoid getting physical before it is safe to do so. The most intimate, personal part of you is thus kept whole. Reserving physical closeness for the security of a permanent relationship helps safeguard your happiness — and your future.

Establishing a Soul Connection

We've seen how saving touch for the right person avoids many pitfalls in relationships. Its main advantage, though, is not what it avoids but what it offers. Two people truly become one by first bringing down the walls, not between their bodies, but between their minds and hearts. This requires a lot of intellectual and emotional sharing — in other words, talking. However, you're less likely to invest hours of your relationship in deep conversation, hoping to feel close, when, at the back of your mind, you know there's a foolproof shortcut: getting physical.

Judaism says: Stop. Wait. Before you let the physical side enter, develop a relationship that stands on its own two feet — a true soul-to-soul connection. Once that relationship is truly solid — after marriage — the physical side will be a beautiful and powerful expression of what you have. There's a big difference between letting sexuality determine an illusory connection and letting it express a real one. Before you give someone the opportunity to appreciate your body, let him or her have the chance to appreciate you for who you truly are. That's the kind of bond that lasts.

By this point in the discussion, most people I discuss *shomer negiah* with can see its benefits. Yet they often point to what they see as the down sides. Let's briefly look at the most common questions that arise.

The Experience Factor

The idea makes sense — passing up on physicality now in order to enhance it later. But what about experience? After all, how else can a person become broad-minded and worldly?

Obviously, to live is to experience. Yet Judaism

urges that experiencing not take place indiscriminately and for its own sake. Most intelligent women don't try being a prostitute just to see what it is like, because we realize that any experience must be sized up for its individual advantages and disadvantages. Experiencing should be a means to an important end: becoming a better and happier person. Some experiences, like the ones in question, simply won't take you where you want to go.

Compatibility

Maybe it won't work on a physical level, and you'll be stuck in a passionless, boring relationship.

People used to fall in love and get married without checking out "compatibility." They had happy, long-lasting marriages this way. It can still work for us.

Maybe they were sexually bored their whole lives and didn't divorce because of the social stigma attached to divorce at that time.

What you're really asking is, "How can you know if the sex will be good without trying it out first?" This whole question rests on a faulty premise. Modern society has made a fatal error in relating to the body independently of the spirit that animates it. This body-soul division has led to sexuality being viewed as a kind of physical skill divorced from the spirit, like tennis. And, after all, would you commit to being someone's lifelong tennis partner if you've never once played with him or her?

The crucial mistake in this approach lies in the very comparison. Sexuality is neither a sport nor a skill — it is a deep and wonderful expression of feelings. People are whole human beings — the body and soul are interconnected and cannot so coldly be separated from each other. I'd say that the emotional connection counts for at least ninety percent of the pleasure and satisfaction you'll experience in your physical relationship. Even if not there initially, the ten percent of technique (the how-to's) can be quickly learned, much like you can tell a close friend where and how hard to scratch your back when it itches. But no matter how good the physical side is, you can't change the person's personality to become someone you mistakenly thought they already were. In essence, when you have a healthy attitude toward sexual expression, love each other, are committed to each other, and want to bring each other pleasure, you have nothing to worry about.

"No Pain, No Gain"

People have to live in the real world. We grow from failures and mistakes — they are part of growing up. Why live in a bubble?

Failures can be powerful learning experiences. But life deals us enough challenges to deal with and mistakes to grow from that we don't need to go looking for more. Considering the toll they take on a person's psyche and the unfortunate memories and comparisons that will harm the ultimate relationship that everyone wants, much of this pain is simply not worth it.

Judaism encourages us to set up a solid foundation for the ultimate relationship each of us wants to develop. It is crucial to maintain your objectivity, avoid emotional scarring, and build a genuine spiritual bond with your partner. Refraining from getting physical accomplishes this. It helps you find the right person and leaves you whole and able to create a deep, trusting, and loving relationship that will last a lifetime. It creates the space for something real to develop and for you to recognize and appreciate the real person you are with.

Author's note: You may admire the beauty behind the idea of being *shomer negiah* but feel that (a) it is too late — you've been physical with others before — and (b) you're not ready for such a major life change. You may then conclude that the concept has little to do with you. Don't. Any step in this direction offers tremendous benefits, whether more objectivity, more sensitization, or just the confidence to make changes that will serve your higher interests in the end.

GILA MANOLSON is a well-known lecturer on Judaism and sexuality. She teaches for the Isralight Institute in the Old City of Jerusalem and is the author of *The Magic Touch: The Jewish Approach to Relationships* and *Outside/Inside: A Fresh Look at Tzniut*. She lives with her husband and family in Jerusalem.

Rebbetzin Tehilla Abramov

The Secret Ingredient of a Successful Marriage

What is the secret, mysterious ingredient necessary for bringing together a couple's disparate personalities? The cementing ingredient is the ultimate in intimacy: physical intimacy.

Physical intimacy is meant to be enjoyable. Thousands of years before Masters and Johnson and the woman's liberation movement, the Jewish tradition recognized the importance of women gaining as much pleasure from physical intimacy as men. One of the obligations of a Jewish husband is to give his wife physical pleasure.

But intimacy is more than just momentary pleasure. Judaism views physical intimacy as the ultimate vehicle to express emotional intimacy, to create closeness. Therefore Jewish law limited it to a framework where emotional bonding is essential. A person engaging in casual expressions of this most personal aspect of life must become desensitized to the emotional dimension of the experience. This desensitization cripples one emotionally and spiritually. When people thus crippled get married, they have difficulty reawakening their sensitivity and achieving true intimacy.

The complete commitment and emotional closeness of marriage allow physical relations to be the most intense, potent, and powerful experience possible. Such an experience is possible when we conserve and reserve all of our sexuality for our spouse.

People were created in such a way that they are meant to be sensitive to every sight, to the slightest touch. Every interaction between husband and wife is meant to be meaningful, even a hand brushing a shoulder. By directing this intimate side of ourselves to one person only, we preserve and enhance it. Sharing this experience with others, whether through speech, dress, or action, dilutes its power. It's a sad truth that we are the most overexposed generation in history.

Since physical relations play a significant role in the cementing of a marriage, it is of paramount importance that they are always meaningful and enjoyable. One of the most commonly encountered problems in marriage is boredom with physical intimacy, which inevitably creates tension and can contribute to the souring of a relationship. Dr. Domeena Renshaw, head of the Sexual Dysfunction Clinic of Chicago's Loyola University, states that 80 percent of the divorces in Western society come about because of dysfunction within the couple's intimate lives. Furthermore, 50 percent of the couples who remain married have problems in this area. Familiarity breeding contempt is certainly a significant factor in these problems.

The most natural solution to such a situation, in order to invigorate the relationship, is a temporary cessation of physical contact. (This does not mean emotional distance.) Researchers experimented with this concept and found that it worked beautifully — in the lab. As soon as the couple went home, though, their self-imposed separation agreement didn't work. They began to find exceptions to the rules they'd created, which brought about confusion, tension, and misunderstanding.

Jewish tradition avoids such ambivalence and ambiguity by employing an objective physiological factor — menstruation — to determine the times of physical closeness and separation. This Divinely ordained system, called "*taharat hamishpachah*" (family purity), mandates a complete cessation of physical contact between husband and wife during the time of the woman's menstrual cycle (a minimum of five days) and for seven days following the cessation of bleeding. The woman checks to ascertain when her period has ended and continues to check that there is no bleeding during the subsequent seven days.

The guesswork is removed; the subtle pressures are eliminated. The onset of the menses signifies a change in status in the relationship, during which time husband and wife are not permitted to have physical relations with one another: they don't sleep in the same bed together, nor do they touch each other. Because it is total, the separation enhances physical intimacy when they join together. The goal of this system is to increase awareness and appreciation of physical expressions, making every touch count. Even a good-night kiss should not be a perfunctory ritual, but an expression of love and desire.

Too often, a couple uses physical expression to hide the lack of emotional connection underneath. The physical distance mandated by *taharat hamishpachah* enables the couple to focus on other methods of interaction. The distance gives them space to communicate on a different level and to be friends with each other. This emphasis on communication then carries over into the time when there is no separation, creating emotional intimacy. Couples who follow this Jewish law find it the glue that holds their relationship together, even when they observe no other Jewish law.

The period of separation also gives us an opportunity

for individuality, a period of privacy within the total to-
getherness of marriage. And it reflects respect for the
woman's biological well-being. A woman's vaginal dis-
charges are slightly acidic and serve as a natural barrier to
infection. During her period, this discharge shifts to alka-
line, and the natural barrier is lost. It takes about a week
for the normal acidity to be restored. The uterine channel
is also in a vulnerable state, having shed the protective
uterine lining, and it takes seven days from the end of
menstruation for this lining to re-form. Thus, research
has shown, a woman is more susceptible to infection
during her period and for the seven days following.

Dr. Alexander Gunn, a renowned British researcher,
published the following: "Jewish principles which require couples to abstain from intercourse for a certain
number of days after the end of menstruation may be
playing their part in protecting the woman. The cells on
the surface of the cervix are known to be most susceptible to damage just after menstruation." This explains
another study which has shown that women who observe *taharat hamishpachah* are twenty times less likely
to suffer from cervical cancer than women who do not
observe these laws.

But the separation, ultimately, is a means to an end.
It is intended to build emotional closeness between husband and wife so that when they do come together
physically they can express this closeness to the utmost.
Marital relations are a physical culmination of a relationship which in its totality should be loving, caring,
and emotionally fulfilling.

At the end of seven spotless days the woman bathes
thoroughly so she can immerse in the mikveh, a collection of natural waters. This immersion is not intended
to cleanse. Rather, the woman, passing through these
waters, once again changes her status and joins her husband intimately.

The symbolism of the mikveh is multifaceted. The mikveh waters are called *mayim chayim*, "living waters." Water sustains all life; from the rain on the crops to the water in our cells, we are all nourished by water. Thus, at the moment when a couple can renew physical relations, the woman passes through the mikveh as a kind of rebirth. And because the mikveh also symbolizes the rivers of Eden, it serves as a reconnection with the ultimate Source of life and with the spiritual perfection symbolized by the Garden of Eden.

When the woman returns home from the mikveh, she and her husband rejoice in each other and their renewed physical contact. In fact, having marital relations is termed the "commandment of joy." After the separation, this reunion is intended to be a loving, passionate expression of the couple's feelings. It is the wedding night all over again, a rediscovery of each other. With such a cycle of physical separation and reunion, bound together with the thread of emotional connection, a Jewish couple has the key to the golden chain that has enabled the Jewish people to survive through the centuries.

Tourists to Massada, the mountaintop desert fortress in Israel where a group of Jews made a last-ditch effort some two thousand years ago to resist the Romans, are often amazed upon seeing the several ancient *mikva'ot* that were built by these desperate and beleaguered Jews who, despite their dire circumstances, observed *taharat hamishpachah*. But it should come as no surprise — the observance of *taharat hamishpachah* is central to being Jewish. The act of faith embodied in the wife using the mikveh in order to rejoin physically with her husband is the most powerful ritual in Judaism, because it is the factor that has bound the Jewish family together through millennia. And the Jewish family is the heart and soul of the Jewish people.

REBBETZIN TEHILLA ABRAMOV is a world-renowned educator who specializes in the field of marriage and family life. She is the author of the bestselling and acclaimed *The Secret of Jewish Femininity: Insights into the Practice of Taharat HaMispachah*, and *Straight from the Heart: A Torah Perspective on Mothering Through Nursing*. With her husband Rabbi Yirmiyohu Abramov, she has also written *Our Family, Our Strength: Creating a Jewish Home, Two Halves of a Whole: Torah Guidelines for Marriage* and *Harmony in the Home: An Educational Program for the Jewish Family* (all published by Targum Press). Together they are the founders of Jewish Marriage Education (JME: POB 43206, Jerusalem 91431), a nonprofit international organization dedicated to bringing a deeper understanding of marriage and family life to the Jewish community. Due to popular demand, this essay (written in collaboration with her husband) has been reprinted from *Jewish Matters*.

Rebbetzin Rivkah Slonim

Mikveh: Gateway to Purity

Superficially, a modern-day mikveh looks very much like a miniature swimming pool. In a religion rich with detail, beauty, and ornamentation — against the backdrop of the ancient Temple or even the contemporary synagogue — the mikveh is surprisingly nondescript, a humble structure.

Its ordinary appearance, however, belies its primary place in Jewish life and law. The mikveh offers the individual, the community, and the nation of Israel the remarkable gift of purity and holiness. No other religious establishment, structure, or rite can affect the Jew in this way and on such an essential level. Its extraordinary power has held sway since the dawn of time.

Our tradition relates that after being banished from Eden, Adam sat in a river that flowed from the garden as part of his attempt to return to his original perfection. Before the revelation at Sinai, all Jews were commanded to immerse themselves in preparation for coming face to face with God. In the desert, the famed well of Miriam served as a mikveh, and Aaron and his sons' induction into the priesthood was marked by immersion in the mikveh. In Temple times, the priests as well as each Jew who wished entry into the House of God had to first immerse in a mikveh. On Yom Kippur, the holiest of all days, the high priest was allowed entrance into the Holy of Holies, the innermost chamber of the Temple, into which no other mortal could enter. This was the zenith of a day that involved an ascending order of services — each of which was preceded by immersion in the mikveh.

The primary uses of mikveh today are delineated in Jewish law and date back to the dawn of Jewish history. They cover many elements of Jewish life. Mikveh is an integral part of conversion to Judaism. Mikveh is used for the immersion of new pots, dishes, and utensils before they may be used by a Jew. The mikveh concept is also the focal point of the purification rite of a Jew before the person is laid to his eternal rest and the soul descends on high. Men may use the mikveh on various occasions; with the exception of conversion they are all customary. The most widely practiced customs are immersion by a groom on his wedding day and by every man before Yom Kippur. But the most important and general usage of mikveh is for purification by the menstruant woman within a framework known as *taharat hamishpachah*, family purity.

The observance of family purity, and immersion in the mikveh within that framework, is a biblical injunction of the highest order. While most Jews see the synagogue as the central institution in Jewish life, Jewish law states that constructing a mikveh takes precedence over building a house of worship. Both a synagogue and a Torah scroll, Judaism's most venerated treasure, may be sold to raise funds for the building of a mikveh. In the eyes of Jewish law, a group of Jewish families living together do not attain the status of a community if they do not have access to a mikveh. Jewish married life, and therefore the birth of future generations in accordance with Jewish law, is possible only where there is accessibility to a mikveh. It is clearly no exaggeration to state that the mikveh is the touchstone of Jewish life and the portal to a Jewish future.

Separation

The concept of mikveh is rooted in the spiritual. Jewish life is marked by the notion of *havdalah*, separation and distinction. On Saturday night, as the Shabbat departs and the new week begins, Jews are reminded of the borders that delineate every aspect of life. Over a cup of wine, we bless God, Who "separates between the holy and the mundane, between light and darkness, between Israel and the nations, between the seventh day and the six days of labor...." In fact, the literal definition of the Hebrew word *kodesh*, most often translated as "holy," is "that which is separated." In many ways, mikveh is the threshold separating the unholy from the holy, but it is even more.

Simply put, immersion in a mikveh signals a change in status — more correctly, an elevation in status. Utensils that could heretofore not be used can, after immersion, be utilized in the holy act of eating as a Jew. A woman who from the onset of her menses was in a state of *niddut*, separated from her husband, may after immersion be reunited with him in the ultimate holiness of married intimacy. Men or women in Temple times, who were precluded from services because of ritual defilement, could, after immersion, enter the House of God. The case of the convert is most dramatic. The individual who descends into the mikveh as a gentile emerges from beneath its waters as a Jew. While an understanding of the ultimate reason of any of God's commandments is impossible, there are insights that can add meaning to our mikveh experience.

Purity

In the beginning, there was only water. A miraculous compound, it is the primary source and vivifying factor of all sustenance and, by extension, all life as we know it. But it is more. For these very same attributes — water as source and sustaining energy — are mirrored in the spiritual. Water has the power to purify, to restore and replenish life to our essential, spiritual selves. The mikveh personifies both the womb and the grave, the portals to life and the afterlife. In both, the person is stripped of all power and prowess. In both, there is a mode of total reliance, complete abdication of control.

Immersion in the mikveh can be understood as a symbolic act of self-abnegation, the conscious suspension of the self as an autonomous force. In so doing, the person immersing signals a desire to achieve oneness with the Source of all life, God. Immersion indicates the abandonment of one form of existence to embrace one infinitely higher. It is thus described not only in terms of purification, revitalization, and rejuvenation but also — and perhaps primarily — as rebirth.

In primitive societies, menstruating women were a source of consternation and fear. Peace could be made with menstruation only by ascribing it to evil and demonic spirits and by the adaptation of a social structure that facilitated its avoidance. Viewed against this backdrop, the Jewish rhythm in marriage is perceived by many as a throwback to archaic taboos, a system rooted in antiquated attitudes and a ubiquitous form of misogyny.

In truth, family purity is a celebration of life and our most precious human relationships. It can be understood most fully only within a deeper notion of purity and impurity.

Judaism teaches that the source of all *taharah*, purity, is life itself. Conversely, death is the harbinger of *tumah*, impurity. All types of ritual impurity, and the Torah describes many, are rooted in the absence of life or some measure — even a whisper — of death.

When stripped to its essence, a woman's menses signals the death of potential life. Each month a woman's body prepares for the possibility of conception. The uterine lining is built up — rich and replete, ready to serve as a cradle for life — in anticipation of a fertilized ovum. Menstruation is the shedding of the lining, the end of this possibility. The presence of potential life within fills a woman's body with holiness and purity. With the departure of this potential, impurity sets in, conferring upon the woman a state of impurity or, more specifically, *niddut*. Impurity is neither evil nor dangerous, and it is not something tangible. Impurity is a spiritual state of being, the absence of purity, much as darkness is the absence of light. Only immersion in the mikveh, following the requisite preparation, has the power to change the status of the woman.

The concept of purity and impurity as mandated by the Torah and applied within Jewish life is unique; it has no parallel or equivalent in this postmodern age. Perhaps that is why it is difficult for the contemporary mind to relate to the notion and view it as relevant. In ancient times, however, *tumah* and *taharah* were central and determining factors. The status of a Jew, whether he or she was ritually pure or impure, was at the very core of Jewish living. It dictated and regulated a person's involvement in all areas of ritual.

Most notably, *tumah* made entrance into the Holy Temple impossible. There were numerous types of impurities that affected Jews — regarding both their life and Temple service — and a commensurate number of purification processes. Mikveh immersion was the culmination of the purification rite in every case. Even for the ritually pure, ascending to a higher level of spiritual involvement or holiness necessitated immersion in a mikveh. As such, the institution of mikveh took center stage in Jewish life. In our day, in this post-Temple period, the power and interplay of ritual status has all but vanished, relegating this dynamic to obscurity.

There is, however, one arena in which purity and impurity continue to be pivotal. In this connection only is there a biblical mandate for mikveh immersion — and that is regarding human sexuality. Human love-making signals the possibility and potential for new life, the formation of a new body and the descent from Heaven of a new soul. In their fusing, man and woman become part of something larger; in their transcendence of the self, they draw on, and even touch, the Divine. They enter into a partnership with God; they come closest to taking on the Godly attribute of creator. In fact, the sacredness of the intimate union remains unmitigated even when the possibility of conception does not exist. In the metaphysical sense, the act and its potential remain linked.

Human sexuality is a primary force in the lives of a married couple; it is the unique language and expression of the love they share. A strong relationship between husband and wife is not only the backbone of their own family unit but is integral to the world at large. The blessings of trust, stability, continuity, and, ultimately, community all flow from the commitment they have to each other and to a joint future. In reaffirming their commitment, in their intimacy, the couple adds to the vibrancy and health of their society and to the fruition of the Divine plan: a world perfected by man. As such, they are engaged in the most sacred of pursuits.

In this light, it becomes clear why marital relations are often referred to as the holy temple of human endeavor. And entrance to the holy always was, and continues to be, contingent on ritual purity.

While we cannot presently serve God in a physical Temple in Jerusalem, we can erect a sacred shrine within our lives. Immersion in the mikveh is the gateway to the holy ground of conjugality.

Blessings

The mikveh cycle, also known as the laws of family purity, is a Divine ordinance. There is no better or more legitimate reason for their observance. And therein lies the mitzvah's potency. The knowledge that it is sourced in something larger than the self — that it is not based on the emotions or a subjective decision — allows *taharat hamishpachah* to work for the mutual benefit of woman and husband. Ironically, this "unfathomable" mitzvah reveals its blessings to us more than almost any other in daily, palpable ways.

At first glance, the mikveh system speaks of limitations and constraints — a loss of freedom. In truth, emancipation is born of restriction. Secure, confident, well-adjusted children (and adults) are disciplined children; they understand restraint and ultimately learn self-control. Safe, stable countries are those pieces of land surrounded by definite, well-guarded borders. The drawing of parameters creates terra firma amid chaos and confusion and allows for traversing the plain we call life in a progressive and productive manner. And in no area of life is this more necessary than in our most intimate relationships.

Over time, open-ended sexual availability often leads to a waning of excitement and even interest. Mikveh's monthly hiatus teaches couples to treasure the time they have together. They count the days until they can be together, and each time there is a new quality to their reunion. In this regard, the Talmud states, "So that she will be as beloved as on the day of her marriage." In this way, they are constantly involved in an ongoing process of becoming "one flesh."

Furthermore, human beings share a nearly universal tendency for the forbidden. How many otherwise intelligent individuals have jeopardized their marriages and families in pursuit of the illicit because of its seeming promise of the romantic and the new? Mikveh introduces a novel scenario: one's spouse — one's partner in life, day after day, for better and for worse — becomes temporarily inaccessible, forbidden, off limits.

For many women, their time as a *niddah* also offers them a measure of solitude and introspection. There is, additionally, an empowering feeling of autonomy over their bodies and, indeed, over the sexual relationship they share with their spouses. There is strength and comfort in the knowledge that human beings can neither have their every whim nor be had at whim.

The benefits brought to married life by the practice of family purity have been recognized by numerous experts, Jew and gentile alike. Ultimately, however, mikveh's powerful hold on the Jewish people — its promise of hope and redemption — is rooted in the Torah and flows from a belief in God and His perfect wisdom. Judaism calls for the consecration of human sexuality. It is not enough that intimacy be born of commitment and sworn to exclusivity; it must be sacred. By immersing in the mikveh, each woman can link herself to an ongoing tradition that has spanned the generations. Through mikveh she brings herself in immediate contact with the Source of life, purity, and holiness — with the God who surrounds her and is within her always.

REBBETZIN RIVKAH SLONIM is education director of the Chabad House Jewish Student Center in Binghamton, New York, and an internationally known teacher, activist, and lecturer with a special focus on women in Jewish law and life. She is the author of the acclaimed book *Total Immersion: A Mikveh Anthology* (Jason Aronson Inc., 1996), from which this essay is adapted, and a consultant to educators on the subject of mikveh and Jewish family life.

Speaking about...
Jewish Women, Past

"What was I going to pass on to my kids? I want to keep the Jewish tradition alive in our family. It is a beautiful chain going back such a long time, and I'm not going to be the one to end it. I want my kids to be more Jewish than I was. I'll know it won't die out from my family." — Barbara, 40

"When I made my home kosher, I thought of my grandmother and her parents. If they were still here, they'd be so proud of me! And they would eat in my home, too." — Sara, 24

"I came to understand where I am from. I came to see that the greatest source of wisdom and kindness that I knew, my grandmother, was not placed here by Martians. She was not a freak accident born in a test tube. My grandma, who I thought was unique, was in fact a product of a religion and a culture I knew very little about. And her greatness came directly from this Jewish world. So the person I loved most in the world, my grandmother, was a product of something, and I'm a product of it, too." — Carlie, 25

"We all belong to a wonderful people with a long tradition and a strong sense of group identity. We are so lucky." — Laurie, 18

"I think Jewish women should be proud of who they are and where they are coming from. Judaism allows a woman to be a woman with all the dignity and respect she deserves. If you look at the big picture, there is far more respect for women in Judaism than outside it." — Riva, 35

Rebbetzin Leah Kohn

Sarah: Finding the Spiritual in the Mundane

A superficial glance at the Torah might suggest that Abraham was the central figure in early Judaism and that Sarah was his "sidekick." Yet Jewish sources (see *Rashi* and other commentaries on Genesis 16:2; *Bereishit Rabbah* 39:15, 41:2, 60:15; and many other references in the Talmud, Midrash, and later texts) reveal that she was in fact a full partner and a woman of great insight and influence who developed a particularly close and deep relationship with God.

The matriarchs and patriarchs are compared to the roots of a tree; they established the foundation for us. In fact, tradition tells us that everything that happened to them has a parallel within our history. Just as everything the tree becomes has its source in the roots, so everything the Jewish nation becomes and is has its source in the lives of our matriarchs and patriarchs.

Therefore, when faced with a challenge, we are able to examine how they handled adversity and try to emulate their ways. Their examples remain a source of strength for all generations.

In examining the life of Sarah, one must (as always) keep in mind that the Torah is not a history book;

rather, it is a guide for life and therefore shares only those events that are important for our spiritual growth.

Interestingly, the longest discourse about Sarah concerns her death and burial. Such detailed treatment of this subject is unique in Jewish text; it is even surprising in this case because there is a great deal to tell about Sarah's life (for example, the fact that she brought tens of thousands to monotheism) that the written Torah doesn't tell us about. However, it is this passage that unlocks the essence of her greatness.

Jewish law is explicit about proper burial practices. These rituals emphasize respect for the body, because the body is the tool we use in our lifetimes to accomplish our missions in the world. Sarah mastered the use of her body as an instrument of spirituality. That the Torah goes to great lengths in recounting Abraham's negotiation and purchase of the site where her body would rest signifies its perfect utilization in her lifetime.

This accomplishment is also apparent from another incident written about Sarah's life: her experience in Egypt. Taken captive by Pharaoh, her test was overwhelming. She found herself at Pharaoh's side, with access to what was then the world's most advanced, alluring, and cultured civilization, yet at the same time paganistic and immoral. Throughout this test, Sarah remained unaffected in body, mind, and spirit. She did not let the surrounding materialism dominate her; rather, she had pity for the individuals who had access to such an array of resources but didn't utilize them for the right purpose.

Sarah's unwavering commitment to sanctifying every aspect of life remains a Jew's central purpose to this day, and Sarah is *the* role model for fulfilling this goal. She did not differentiate between mundane and holy. She elevated the mundane and made it holy. Sarah utilized everything and every action in life to enhance her relationship with God, even in the midst of the most challenging circumstances.

In recognition of her ability to transform the earthly realm into a dwelling place for the Divine, God bestowed Sarah's home with three miracles. Her Shabbat candles burned all week long, her challah (bread) was blessed with a Divine satiating quality, and the Presence of God hung over her tent in the form of a cloud. Each of these physical manifestations had its counterpart in later Jewish history and has a spiritual significance that remains a force in our lives today.

Our Shabbat candles burn for only a few hours, leaving us without their unique light for the rest of the week. Six days a week we are busy working and providing for our basic needs. The Shabbat candles mark a departure from this routine, ushering in a singular day of focused connection to God.

For Sarah, there was no such separation between holy and mundane. Her clarity did not ebb and flow with the coming and going of Shabbat, and so symbolically her candles burned from one Shabbat to the next. In much the same way, one of the lamps on the Menorah in the Temple never burned out. This suspension of natural law indicated that God had deemed the Temple fitting for His Presence. Sarah was the first to usher God into the physical world in this fashion.

Sarah's challah also expressed how she redefined the boundaries of the physical world by infusing it with spirituality. God embedded a blessing in her challah, which caused it to be completely satisfying no matter how little a guest ate. This bypassed the laws of nature and gave way to a more expansive sense of the physical realm's ultimate, unlimited source. By giving the challah spiritual characteristics, God acknowledged Sarah's ability to use material existence as a pipeline to the Divine. Later in Jewish history, the bread baked in the

Temple remained miraculously fresh throughout the week. This was God's indication that the legacy of spirituality established by Sarah had endured.

The third miracle in Sarah's midst — the cloud of the Divine Presence that hovered over her home — was a clear visual link between Heaven and earth. Regardless of time of day or change in weather, it persisted as proof of a spiritual domain beyond the five senses. This Divine cloud was present because Sarah sanctified every aspect of physical life, a concept also symbolized by (among other things) Sarah's observance of the laws of mikveh, thus infusing her physical body with spirituality. A symbol of God's Presence, the cloud reappeared at key points in the development of the Jewish nation — as a protective force for the generation in the desert and as a sign of the Divine Presence at the giving of the Torah at Mount Sinai.

We no longer live in an era of open miracles such as those fostered by Sarah or those that were present at the Temple. Yet the mitzvot of candle lighting, taking challah (which entails separating a small piece from a certain amount of bread dough and destroying it to symbolize the challah gift that was required to be given to the priest in the Temple era), and mikveh indicate our desire to elevate the physical world and make it spiritual.

Furthermore, each time we use the physical for a higher purpose, we create in ourselves a dwelling place for God. In this way, physicality never becomes an end unto itself. Rather, for the Jew, this world remains a place where the mundane and routine present opportunities to connect to our Source. This task is a challenge, especially when taken on in the midst of a consumer society that overwhelms us with materialistic messages. As Jewish women, we have the potential to walk the path of Sarah, transforming and infusing meaning into every physical aspect of our existence, each in our own way, on our own time, step by step.

REBBETZIN LEAH KOHN is the cofounder and director of the Jewish Renaissance Center, a unique learning institution in Manhattan exclusively for Jewish women with little or no background who wish to learn about Judaism. A twelfth-generation Jerusalemite, she has over thirty years of experience in teaching and directing schools in Israel and the United States.

Natalie Douek

Rebecca: A Sensitive Soul

When Abraham was commanded to sacrifice his beloved son Isaac, Isaac did not protest. He was ready and willing to offer his life for God. Such a personality needed a wife who was also self-sacrificing, who could give of herself to others.

There is a big difference between a person who does good deeds and a person whose very essence is dedicated to helping people. When Abraham and Sarah's servant Eliezer arrived at a well in his search for a wife for Isaac, Rebecca approached and, seeing an opportunity to give, gave both him and his camels water to drink. By doing this, she showed that her very essence was kindness. She could have just helped Eliezer and let him deal with his own camels. After all, she had already helped a stranger — many would have left at that point, proud of the good deed they had just done. But Rebecca didn't stop there. She realized that Eliezer was tired and was sensitive to the fact that his animals were also thirsty.

The commentator known as the Beis HaLevi carefully analyzes her actions toward Eliezer in order to appreciate her greatness. He explains that Rebecca gave from her only jug to a stranger whose cleanliness was doubtful. Afterward, to avoid offending Eliezer by pouring out the water from the jug and rinsing it, she gave the remaining water to the camels, and even offered to continue drawing water for him to show that she was not just getting rid of the remaining water. We see that Rebecca's sensitivity lay in the fact that she perceived the needs of others and did her utmost to fulfill them. Not only was she concerned with others' physical needs, but also with their feelings.

Perhaps the most admirable thing about Rebecca is that she was able to maintain this level of sensitivity coming from a town of swindlers and a home where her father and brother illustrated extreme selfishness and self-interest. Her brother was so insensitive that he could not be happy about his sister's future marriage but was selfishly absorbed in what he could get out of it. Her father was not only unwilling to sacrifice anything for his daughter's happiness, but thought only of his personal financial gain. Considering the huge influence that surroundings have on a person, the fact that she succeeded in acquiring and maintaining this sensitivity to others is all the more impressive.

Why did our matriarch Rebecca have to grow up in such a negative environment? The commentator known as the Tiferes Tzion explains that it was for us. Our matriarchs' and patriarchs' lives were a microcosm of the Jewish people's history. Whatever occurred to them and their reactions to the events would have an impact on all future generations. Therefore Rebecca's life had a direct influence on the Jewish people. Her growing up in a negative environment and yet emerging from it with a sense of righteousness and goodness intact gave us the ability to withstand and grow even in such harsh environments and plant within us a strong desire and love for kindness no matter what the circumstance.

This is Rebecca's legacy to us.

NATALIE DOUEK is a tutor for Ohr Somayach's Jewish Learning Exchange in London, England, and a participant in the JLE Gesharim training program. She wrote this essay with the help and encouragement of Rebbetzin Joanne Dove, director of Women's Programming at the JLE.

Nechama Dina Kumer and the Ascent staff

Rachel: A Call for Compassion

Among all of the matriarchs, Rachel is unique. She is the only one not buried in the family cave in Hebron. The Torah relates that her burial place is "on the way to Efrat in Bethlehem." What are we supposed to learn from this?

The matriarchs were prophetesses whose level of prophecy sometimes surpassed even that of their mates. Rachel understood that generations later her children were to be exiled from the Holy Land, and she prepared for it and gave up her rightful burial place in Hebron.

Hundreds of years later, when the exile actually happened, the prophet Jeremiah accompanied the nation on their tragic journey and beseeched God for mercy and that their punishment be lessened. The merit of the forefathers, and even Moses himself, was not enough to change the decree. When Rachel wept on their behalf that they be returned once again to their land as they passed her burial site in Bethlehem, God answered Rachel's prayers. Her prayer had the effect of arousing God's compassion for His errant nation.

What was so unique about Rachel's plaint that she received the desired response more than the other righteous leaders?

The Hebrew word *rachel* means "sheep." Of all the animals, a sheep is the most passive. A sheep's will is in-

stinctively nullified before the shepherd's. Yet even the
toughest shepherd succumbs with mercy to the helpless
bleat of a sheep. Because Rachel realized her potential in
nullifying her will, even after her passing she was able to
come to the aid of her people by arousing God's compassion. It was for this reason that Rachel selflessly gave
up her place of burial in Hebron when God decreed that
her time on earth was to end.

Rachel was the cornerstone of Jacob's household. It
was Rachel for whom Jacob toiled for fourteen years so
he could marry her. Jacob was the spiritual leader and
prophet of his generation. The obvious place for Rachel's burial would be at his side, in Hebron. But Jacob
knew of Rachel's desire to be buried in Bethlehem, and
he fulfilled her wish. Not only did Jacob know that Rachel was willing to give up this eternal honor for the
sake of her children, but he knew she felt truly joyous to
do so. She knew that in burial she would remain isolated
for thousands of years for the sake of descendants who
would live generations afterward. She knew these future
offspring would have little merit. And still she sacrificed
for them with joy!

This is true self-nullification. This is Rachel. In the
face of this utter selflessness lasting millennia, God responded with compassion. Her tearful prayers bore
fruit. "Your deeds are rewarded," God answered her cry.
The Jews would be returned to Israel. Their redemption
came before her personal honor.

How can we connect to this spiritual giant?

Woman and Malchut

According to kabbalah, there are ten spheres of Divine influence, ten levels through which God's bounty
is filtered down to the world. Rachel corresponds to the
last of the spiritual spheres, *Malchut*, Kingship. This

sphere is uniquely known as the "recipient sphere" because, being on the bottom rung, so to speak, it receives the spiritual influences of the preceding nine spheres. In order to be a receptor for their influence, *Malchut* humbles and nullifies its identity.

But this is not the full picture by any means. *Malchut* also actualizes and transmits this influence into the physical world of finite beings who live their existence within time, space, and dimension. *Malchut*, in a way, is the intermediary between the higher spiritual realms and the material world.

This is why the attribute associated with *Malchut* is speech. Speech is a way of revealing externally what is hidden in the mind and soul. Similarly, what only exists in potential within the other spheres is revealed by *Malchut*. When Rachel spoke and her "voice was heard on high" (Jeremiah 31:14), God responded to her request that the Jews be returned to their land. Rachel utilized her well-developed power of *Malchut*, connecting herself directly to Heaven.

The Power of Rachel Is in Every Woman

Understanding Rachel and her relationship to the Jewish nation also helps us understand the unique connection between a Jewish mother and her children. The status of the mother determines the identity of the soul of her child. If she is a Jew, so is her child. Rachel demonstrated this spiritual connection to her future children. Regardless of their merit or sinfulness, she is their essential spiritual source. The bond is absolute and eternal.

All Jewish women possess an inheritance from Rachel. She bequeathed to us the ability to relinquish our wishes and comforts for the sake of redeeming the Jewish nation. This is no small thing. This unique feminine ability knows no bounds. Women have the opportunity to teach other Jews about their identity, tradition, and spirituality. The responsibility is ours for the taking. The task is enormous, but its result is even greater: the final and complete redemption of the entire Jewish nation. As the Talmud says, "In the merit of righteous Jewish women, the Jews were redeemed from Egypt. And it is in their merit that we will be redeemed from the present exile."

> NECHAMA DINA KUMER is a working member of the Ascent Institute of Safed in Israel, a year-round Jewish study/recreation center and travel base in the mountains of northern Israel that serves as a mystical Jewish retreat for individuals and groups from all over the Jewish world. Certainly worth a visit.

Lori Palatnik

Leah and the Lesson of Gratitude

From the day God created the world, there was no one who thanked God until Leah came and thanked Him.

(Berachot 7b)

Leah, married to Jacob, was one of the matriarchs of the Jewish people. In the passage above, the Talmud is referring to the birth of Leah's fourth son, Judah.

Judah's Hebrew name, Yehudah, shares the same root as the word *todah*, meaning "thank you." But how can the Talmud say that Leah was the first person to ever thank God? Abraham never thanked God? Sarah never thanked God? Noah never thanked God?

Of course they did. Many people had thanked God in the Torah long before Leah. The Talmud must be telling us that there was something special about Leah's thankfulness. Her gratitude must have been somehow truer and deeper than that of anyone who had come before her.

By understanding what made Leah's gratitude special, we will learn what true gratefulness is all about.

Seeing Everything as a Gift

Leah was a prophetess who knew that the Jewish nation was destined to descend from the twelve sons of Jacob, her husband. Each tribe would be a foundation stone that would shape our history. Jacob's sons were destined to come from four women: Leah, Rachel, Bilhah, and Zilpah. Since there were to be twelve, Leah expected that each of these four women would have three sons.

Judah was Leah's fourth son. She recognized that he was one more than "her share." Her thankfulness for Judah was deeper and more heartfelt because he was unexpected. He was a gift.

This is how we are supposed to view everything in life. Every ray of sunshine, every child, every breath — they are all gifts from God. The mistake of thinking anything is owed us blocks us from gratitude. People sometimes don't appreciate sight until they meet someone who is blind. We shouldn't wait until we are sick (God forbid) to appreciate our health. We should count our blessings every day and take pleasure in the miraculous gifts bestowed on us.

Beginning the Day with Gratitude

The Jewish tradition teaches that every morning we should rise with the *"Modeh Ani"* prayer on our lips. In it we say that we are grateful to God for reviving us each and every day.

When we lose a loved one, we are forced to stand and face our own mortality. We do not live forever, and we do not know from one day to the next when our time will come. All we can do is say *"Modeh Ani"*: "I am grateful to God for giving me another day and another opportunity to use it wisely."

A Jew is called *"Yehudi"* from the name Yehudah, for

the essence of being a Jew is to be thankful. This is what distinguished Judah, and his mother, from whom he inherited this trait. We must realize, as Leah did, that every moment of life is a gift.

LORI PALATNIK is a teacher with Aish HaTorah in Toronto and the author of two books, *Friday Night and Beyond: The Shabbat Experience Step by Step* (Jason Aronson Inc.) and *Remember My Soul: What to Do in Memory of a Loved One* (Leviathan Press), from which this essay is adapted. Together with her husband, Rabbi Yaakov Palatnik, they run The Village Shul, an outreach synagogue in Toronto's Forest Hill, and raise five terrific kids. Plans for the future include a move to Boca Raton, Florida, where they plan to open up a new branch of Aish HaTorah. Mrs. Palatnik is also known as a dynamic speaker and has addressed groups throughout North America, illuminating traditional Jewish wisdom for our contemporary world.

Barbara Horwitz

Miriam's Lesson

Miriam, the sister of Moses and one of the seven prophetesses mentioned in the Torah, not only demonstrated a tremendous amount of vision and faith in God, but is also credited with saving the Jewish people on more than one occasion.

As a little girl living during the Egyptian enslavement, Miriam witnessed Pharaoh's decree that all male infants be cast into the river. Her father, Amram, was so upset by the thought of innocent Jewish boys being sentenced to death that he separated from his wife. Who could bring children into such a world? Who could risk their murder? Since Amram was then the leader of the Jewish people, his example was followed, and soon the future of the Jewish people was endangered.

Young Miriam had faith that God would not abandon His people. She respectfully approached her father and said, "Pharaoh has made a decree against the male infants, but you have also decreed against the female children."

Amram immediately saw the error of his ways and reunited with his wife. Several months later, Moses, the greatest Jewish leader of all of history, was born. The other families followed suit, and the Jewish people survived.

Interestingly, Miriam's name comes from the word

mar, which means "bitter." With her birth, the enslavement became much harder, and many believed her to have brought bad tidings (many even called her Bish Gada, which means "bad luck"). She told them to call her Mazal Tov, meaning "good luck," for after the distress would come the redemption, just like after the pains of labor comes the birth itself.

Of course she was correct. After a difficult enslavement, the Jews were finally granted their freedom. Despite their extreme haste to leave Egypt, Miriam instructed the women to take drums and tambourines with them on the journey. It seemed like such an extraneous item at the time, but Miriam was demonstrating and teaching incredible faith to the Jewish women that the nation would soon be redeemed, bringing them the opportunity to sing praise to God with their instruments.

Sure enough, God split the sea for the Jewish people. Then the famous Song of the Sea was sung, while Miriam took the women aside to express an even more exalted level of praise through their instruments.

Despite a terrible enslavement and Pharaoh's wicked decree, Miriam continuously focused on the future. Her lesson to us all is that we should never give up. Difficulties arise, but if we will only hold on and not lose hope, changes for the better are sure to come.

BARBARA HORWITZ, an alumna of Neve Yerushalayim College for Women in Jerusalem, is a full-time journalist living in Chicago and often writes for many the city's Jewish organizations, namely, Yeshivat Migdal Torah, the Chicago Community Kollel, and the Chicago Torah Network. She has published articles in many Jewish publications, including the *Chicago JUF News*, *Washington Jewish Week*, the *Detroit Jewish News*, *Jewish Action*, and *Horizons* magazine.

Rebbetzin Tzipora Heller

Ruth and Two Paths to Spirituality

> Where you go, I will go, and where you stay, I
> will stay. Your people will be my people, and
> your God my God.
>
> (Ruth 1:16)

Ruth was a princess from the country of Moab who became the role model for converts to Judaism. She was so sincere that she merited to have King David as her great-grandson and to have her story become part of the Hebrew Bible. In her old age, she sat in a special, honored seat to the right of her great-great-grandson King Solomon. In order to understand her accomplishments and their meaning for us today, we must look at the society in which she grew up.

Jews are supposed to strive to express the traits of compassion, shame, and kindness. The Moabites personified the complete opposite. They were cruel, shameless, and performed no acts of kindness to speak of. In order to win a war, they sent out their own daughters to seduce and weaken the enemy. They refused to give bread and water to needy Jews passing through the desert.

Furthermore, Jews are essentially spiritual, trying to

elevate themselves and the whole world. The Moabites were completely materialistic, looking out only for themselves. With this understanding, the exemplary Jew who Ruth became is much more striking.

Because of a famine in Israel, Ruth's future husband and his family came to live in Moab. But knowing what we do about that country, why did they go there? Surely there were plenty of other places to go.

Although it may have been convenient, this choice reveals that he and his family may have been affected by the material property of Moab to the point of compromising their spiritual potential. The lowliness of the surrounding society didn't bother them. From the point of view of Ruth's husband, moving to Moab and marrying a Moabite woman was a move in the wrong direction, leading to immorality and materialism.

Yet from Ruth's point of view, marrying him was the best move she could make. She realized that there were sparks of goodness present in her and decided to relate to them and build on them. By marrying into the Jewish people (even though her husband was not a model Jew), she connected herself to a sense of spirituality and goodness that was completely lacking in her society. She raised herself high above where she started. In order to do so, Ruth concentrated on the good in herself and in the people she was exposed to in order to learn and improve.

We have seen how Ruth attached herself to goodness. Jewish mysticism teaches that there is a second path to holiness that focuses on analyzing evil in order to avoid it.

We can best understand this through a recent example. There was a great chassidic Jew known as the Klausenberger Rebbe, *zt"l*, who underwent horrors during the Holocaust. He survived, rebuilt his life, and established a hospital in the town of Netanya so that local residents could have quality health care. The project required an enormous amount of fund-raising, which was very difficult for him in his old age. Why go to all the trouble? He explained that he made one resolution during the war: Whatever the Nazis were, I won't be. They extinguished life; I'll save life. They were cruel; I'll dedicate my life to acts of kindness. He focused on the evil in order to know what not to be.

Ruth took both paths. She saw the good and moved toward it, and she recognized the bad and distanced herself from it — to the point of leaving the decadent Moab and coming to the Land of Israel after her husband's death. Through these two paths, she succeeded in raising herself to incredibly high levels of spirituality. The fact that her story is in one of the books of the Hebrew Bible means that we can learn from her example. Every single one of us has the capacity to follow her path, to grow in the ways she did.

A biography of the author can be found on page 27.

Nicole Landau

Esther's Choice

At a glance, the story of Purim is fantastical, whimsical even, a coincidence-ridden fanciful tale that one really wants to believe. The king kills his queen. Esther ascends to the throne. Her uncle Mordechai overhears a scheme to kill the king, saves him, and in the end Esther and Mordechai together save the Jewish people. On the surface, these seem like disconnected, random events. And where, we ask, is God in all of this?

Learning a little about Esther may help us answer this question. The verses tell us of what happened when Esther was first brought before the king as a candidate for becoming the new queen:

> Now when the turn came for Esther, the daughter of Avichayil, the uncle of Mordechai...to come before the king, she requested nothing....
> (Esther 2:15)

This refers to Esther's refusal to use the cosmetics provided to every candidate for queen. The commentator known as the Menos HaLevi asks why she did this and why her family is mentioned at this point. He explains that instead of being seduced by the material wealth and glory attendant on becoming queen, Esther focused on her spiritual treasure — her heritage. As a result, she did not request makeup in the hope that she would be rejected and sent home to her family. Physical pleasure was not what she sought. To Esther, the deeper, hidden world was far more real.

The very name of the book we read on Purim hints at this idea: Megillas Esther, the Scroll of Esther. In Hebrew, the word *Esther* is related to the word *nistar*, meaning "hidden," and the word *megillah* is related to the word *megaleh*, meaning "to reveal." Thus the Megillah of Esther can be literally translated as "the revelation of that which is hidden." Esther's name and essence are one. She focused on what is important and meaningful, even though it might be hidden from the eye.

Then and now, God's Presence is not readily visible. In fact, God's Name is not mentioned once throughout the entire megillah. Yet Esther makes her choice. She does not perceive the honor of becoming queen as real. She calls on that which is inner, deeper, and hidden. She prays to the God Whom she knows is present. In the face of a decree of extinction hanging over the Jewish people, she calls for a three-day fast, for Esther understands that by temporarily suspending the physical aspects of reality (such as eating), the deeper spiritual world is brought within reach. By initially evading the role of queen by refusing makeup, and later, by risking her position in the palace — and her life — by approaching the king without being summoned, Esther reaches past the physical and dedicates herself to her Jewish identity, inspiring the entire Jewish people, then and now, to do the same.

> NICOLE LANDAU teaches at Ma'ayan Bina, Ohr Somayach's women's seminary in Johannesburg, South Africa. She is also completing her honor's degree in fine art, where she explores Jewish spiritual concepts using sculpture, video, and installation.

Speaking about...
Jewish Women, Present

"I went to the Sufis (Muslim mystics), but they said, "You are Jewish. Go learn about your own religion." — Paula, 19

"I chose to become more involved in my heritage and so started going to shuls and inevitably was invited over for Shabbat meals. Yes, I was a complete stranger, but I was Jewish and 'part of the family' — a huge gift given to me just because my mother is Jewish. And it was so incredible, this Shabbat! I grew up pretty happy, but the singing, the laughter, the stories — where else have I experienced that? People are connected to each other, care for each other, celebrate together, and mourn together. A rabbi even called me just to ask how I was!" — Andrea, 28

"I feel enormous admiration for observant Jewish families. I'm sure you'll find exceptions, but wherever I go I see that they are closer and warmer than other families. The husband and wife respect each other, the men are more involved in child care, family life is a priority for everyone. — Dina, 24

"It's so important to realize that every day is a gift and that we should be grateful for all the good life has to offer. One of the things I am most grateful for is the special gift of Shabbat God gave us. On Shabbat we connect with each other, with God, and with ourselves. Living near the Old City of Jerusalem, we always enjoy the beauty of Shabbat with a table full of guests from around the world. Shabbat meals are special — there's always lots of singing and sharing of the weekly Torah portion. Later on, things get even better. Friday night is open house in our home, and all are welcome to stop by. From the most secular Israelis to tourists to Hebrew University students to parents who are visiting their children to Orthodox Jews in black hats — all are welcome in our home. Looking around our Shabbat table, I understand what true Jewish unity is all about. For those who have been to our home, we hope you will return often. If not, please visit soon! — Bonnie C. (contact via BonnieC@jewishmatters.com)

Sara Rigler

From India to Israel

I was seeking God, so of course I did not look into Judaism. Instead I went to India. It was the heyday of the sixties, during my junior year at Brandeis. I found a guru and started meditating. Near the end of the year, my guru said to me, "You're Jewish. Why don't you investigate Jewish mysticism?"

Jewish mysticism? I had never heard of it. Not in all my years (twelve to be exact) of afternoon and evening Hebrew school, nor during my devout attendance at Shabbat services at our Conservative synagogue, nor during all my wholehearted involvement in my synagogue youth group, of which I served as chapter president and national board member.

Months of meditating in India had convinced me that there was a spiritual dimension to reality, that life held treasures greater than the physical world could offer, and that by following the proper methods I could elevate myself to the ultimate state: God consciousness. If Judaism also could get me to that goal, why not? I had a warm spot in my heart for Judaism. I changed my round-the-world ticket to include a stop in Israel.

A conscientious college student, I began my search in the card catalogue of the Hebrew University library. Under the entry for "mysticism/Jewish," all the books were written by one man, Gershon Scholem, who, as the introduction to one book revealed, lived right there in Jerusalem.

Intrepid, I knocked on the door of his apartment. Professor Scholem, then retired, gave me two hours of his time in his book-lined study. I explained to him, rather naively, that I was not interested in studying Jewish mysticism as an academic subject; rather, I wanted to live it, as I had seen the people of India live their spirituality, making God the primary focus of their lives. Of course, I did not realize that Professor Scholem was the world's leading advocate of kabbalah as an object of study, not as a path of transformation. He shook his head grimly and told me that I would not find what I was looking for, that no kabbalist worth his salt would teach a woman, especially a woman who did not speak Hebrew or Ladino.

The professor did not realize that what I was looking for had already started to germinate in Jerusalem. The first *ba'al teshuvah* yeshiva for English-speaking men and women who did not come from a religious background had sprouted a few months before, to be followed in the seventies and eighties by a forest of such institutions.

Disappointed, I returned to the United States, finished my final year at Brandeis, and gave my parents *nachas* by graduating Phi Beta Kappa and *magna cum laude*. The day after graduation, I joined an ashram, an Indian-style spiritual community, situated on twenty-one acres of woods in eastern Massachusetts.

I stayed there for the next fifteen years.

I meditated three times a day, served as personal secretary to the guru, a sixty-four-year-old Indian woman, taught meditation and Vedanta philosophy when she was absent at our other ashram or in India, headed the publishing department, cooked for the community and the guests once a week, and tended two extensive flower gardens. My life was full and challenging, internally and externally.

The hardest part of life at the ashram was the lack of what our guru disdainfully called "one-on-one relationships." The ideal of Eastern spiritual paths is celibacy. They assert that sexual relationships dissipate spiritual energy and that emotional attachments divert one's exclusive focus on God. For our ashram community, composed mostly of men and women in their twenties, celibacy was a difficult, unrelenting challenge.

Then, in 1984, during my fifteenth year at the ashram, I was disillusioned and unsettled by a series of scandals involving the most prestigious gurus. First the New Age world was shaken by the revelation that the Zen Roshi heading the San Francisco Zen Center had been having an affair with one of his married students. Next came a host of sexual allegations against the revered Swami Muktananda. After that, one guru after another fell like a game of dominos. Hardly a month went by without hearing of a new scandal involving, in the end, almost every major Hindu, Buddhist, and Jain teacher in America. The July 1985 issue of the *Yoga Journal* featured as its cover story "Why Teachers Go Astray: Gurus, Sex, and Spirituality." It included an article on "Sex Lives of the Gurus" by Buddhist teacher Jack Kornfield, who reported on a personal survey he had conducted: "According to this survey — which includes information on fifty-four teachers — sexual relations form a part of the lives of thirty-nine of them.... Significantly, thirty-four of the thirty-nine teachers who are not celibate have had at least occasional sexual relationships with one or more students."

I was devastated. Here I was straining every nerve and muscle to follow the ideal of celibacy, while the most highly regarded proponents of the path couldn't hack it themselves! And what about the issue of truth? Almost all of those thirty-nine teachers publicly espoused the importance of celibacy and pretended to be celibate. Kornfield concluded: "We need to discover how to join sexuality, conscious awareness, and love and how to integrate all parts of ourselves into our spiritual life." His article was a tacit admission that Eastern paths had no formula for accomplishing this.

That same year, we celebrated the birth centenary of Swami Paramananda, the ashram's founder, by inviting speakers from all of the world's religions. Although in previous years the Jewish speaker had been an alternative "rabbi" with a rainbow tallit and a potpourri approach, this time the Jewish speaker was an authentic Orthodox rabbi. Rabbi Joseph Polak (whom I later found out attended under very special circumstances) had the packed Temple of the Universal Spirit swaying to his *nigun* (song without words). He spoke about "love of God, even unto madness," quoting the twelfth-century sage Maimonides. *This is Judaism?* I marveled. In all my years in the Conservative synagogue, I had rarely heard mention of God, let alone love of God. Could this be the same religion?

Rabbi Polak and his wife invited me to their Brookline home for Shabbat. I resisted. Two months passed, but I kept the scrap of paper with their phone number.

Meanwhile, *A Bridge of Dreams*, the book I had been writing for five years, a 640-page biography of Swami Paramananda, was published. The book was well received in the New Age world. Ram Dass wrote an appreciative review in the *New Age Journal*, and the *Yoga Journal* excerpted it as a cover feature.

Amid this flurry of excitement, I went to the Polaks for Shabbat. Then another one. Then strange things started to happen. Leading a meditation service in the "shrine," the ashram's inner sanctum, I suddenly felt like I was suffocating. My breathing became difficult, I started to sweat, and I stared at my watch, waiting for the earliest possible moment I could escape what had previously been my favorite place in the world. I never entered the shrine again. The next day, I was taking my turn washing dishes in the ashram kitchen. Lokaprana, one of the "brothers," entered and fired a critical comment at me. I burst into tears and ran out of the kitchen.

Our guru decided that I was suffering from burnout in the wake of my book's publication. She offered me two months and two thousand dollars to go anywhere in the world I wanted. I went to a travel agency and picked out brochures for Boro-Boro.

A few days later, through the Polaks, I attended a lecture given by Rabbi Dovid Din, who was visiting Boston from New York. He spoke about Judaism as a yoga. He explained that the word for Jewish law, halachah, literally means "walking." Judaism was a path, with a goal — God consciousness. He explained the rituals of eating kosher and keeping Shabbat as spiritual practices. He said that many people who derided kashrut had no problem committing themselves to a vegetarian regime, that many people who called Jewish practices "mindless rituals" devotedly surrendered themselves to Hindu practices. I blushed. I went home to the ashram, threw away my Boro-Boro brochures, and went back to New York to study kabbalah.

The Polaks had told me about another rabbi in New York, Rabbi Meir Fund, who taught classes in kabbalah in Manhattan and Brooklyn. For a month I studied intensively with him. Then Rabbi Fund said to me, "If you really want to learn about Judaism, you have to go to Jerusalem." I stretched my leave of absence, purchased a two-month ticket to Israel, and arranged to study at Neve Yerushalayim, a yeshivah for women with little or no Jewish background.

Rabbi Fund had arranged for me to spend my first

night in Jerusalem with his friends, Tuvia and Chaya, who were chassidim of the Amshenover Rebbe. That night Tuvia announced that he was going to see the Rebbe. He asked me if I wanted to come. Rabbi Fund had told me about the great holiness of the Amshenover Rebbe. I gladly consented to go along.

Now, fourteen years later, it is extremely difficult to get to see the Rebbe, whose reputation for Divinely inspired guidance has spread far. That night in June, I just walked in. When I walked out twenty minutes later, I was flying. I waited for Tuvia on the deserted street below the Rebbe's tiny apartment, dancing in exaltation. "This place is like India in the sixties," I marveled. "It has the enlightened masters and the fellow travelers." The intensity of the spiritual aspiration in the dozen people I had met during my first day in Jerusalem surprised and inspired me. *This is Judaism?* I kept saying to myself.

During the next several weeks, I attended classes at Neve and around the city. I had major issues with Torah Judaism: feminism, universalism, and others. In every class, and sitting privately with teachers more brilliant than any I had known in college, I questioned, challenged, debated, and argued. The answers always came by understanding the contested concept on a deeper plane. Many of my objections were on a sociological level; the answers were always on a spiritual level.

The most attractive element of the Jewish spiritual path was its sanctification of marriage. In other major religions, marriage is considered a concession to human weakness. Judaism, on the contrary, asserts that marriage is the highest state, that the sanctified union between husband and wife affects mystical unions in the upper worlds. This holiness is achieved by adhering to the laws of family purity, which enjoin a couple to virtually practice celibacy for part of each month, then be together in a loving, committed, sexual relationship the other part of the month. I saw this as the best of both worlds. I was amazed that the formula for integrating every part of ourselves into our spiritual life, which the East painfully lacked, could be found in Judaism.

During all my years at the ashram, I had been striving to transcend the world. Judaism insisted on sanctifying the world. Everything in the physical world, I learned, contains sparks of holiness that can be freed by interacting with that object in the way specified by the Torah. Thus, almost all the mitzvot involve using one's body and the physical world. The physical world could be used to elevate myself, and I could elevate the physical world in the process.

How could it be, I wondered, *that Judaism is the world's most hidden religion? Judaism — with its million-dollar-stained glass edifices, its thousand and one national organizations, its hundreds of community newspapers, its vocal leaders at the forefront of every cause — is more hidden than the lost Buddhism of Tibet.*

Gradually I came to realize that the Judaism I had grown up with was all a facade, like the Wild West street I had once seen at Universal Studios. Behind the facade of the bank, the saloon, the hotel, there was...nothing. The elaborate doorways led nowhere. What I was now discovering was an entirely different religion. Not a structure, but rather a very deep diamond mine. The deeper I went, the more gems I discovered. But it was all hidden underground, invisible to passersby.

I had promised my guru that I would be back in time to drive her to a speaking engagement on August 26. Every night, in the post-midnight hours, I would go to the Western Wall to meditate. In the charged atmosphere of the Wall late at night, I was able to meditate deeply. The inner voice I heard kept telling me that I should stay in Jerusalem and take on the practice of Torah.

My conscious self winced at the prospect. I was thirty-seven years old. I had no money and no job prospects (imagine my resumé: *1970–1985 Ashram secretary*). I had no family or friends in Israel. My whole life — my spiritual path, my livelihood, my guru, and all my friends — was at the ashram. But I had spent my entire adult life learning to align myself with the will of God as I perceived it. Now my intuition told me, in no uncertain terms, that it was God's will for me to stay in Jerusalem and learn.

I stayed. I even, by a convoluted set of circumstances, managed to get my guru's blessing for my new life. My father, who had been eager to send me to medical or law school, consented instead to pay my living expenses in Jerusalem for one year while I studied Torah. Six days after the conclusion of that year, I married a musician from California who, it is clear to me, is my soul mate from forever. My first child was born just after my fortieth birthday; my second child, six years later. We live in a nine-hundred-year-old house in the Old City of Jerusalem, five minutes' walk from the Wall. I still struggle with my spiritual challenges, which is the whole purpose for which we human beings are here in this world, but Judaism has brought me closer to God than I have ever been.

Yes, this is Judaism.

SARA RIGLER is a freelance writer and editor who teaches meditation in Jerusalem.

Stephanie's Story

When I was five, I asked my parents, "When can I go to church to talk to God?" At first my parents thought it was cute. However, I soon found myself enrolled in a weekly Yiddish class. Being a shy child, I did not do well and eventually was asked to leave the class; hence the end of my Yiddish education. I suppose I thought God wasn't in my Yiddish class.

When I was ten, my grandpa died. As the eldest child, I always felt we had a special love for one another. Was my grandfather alone now? I wondered. Did he think of us? Did he know how much I loved him? In my bed that evening, looking up at the ceiling, I cried and asked God to please tell my grandpa that I loved him and missed him. I also added something quite peculiar for a Jewish child, probably picked up from our non-Jewish neighbors: I asked Jesus that just in case he was Messiah, would he please hold my grandpa in his arms and take care of him until I got to Heaven. You see, I wanted to cover all my bases.

Soon after, I asked my parents if I could go to temple and learn about God. I learned to read Hebrew and studied for my bat mitzvah. I eventually met with the rabbi and remember reviewing the English portion of my haftarah. My Torah portion talked about angels, and during one of my sessions with him, the rabbi asked me if I really believed in miracles and angels. I hesitantly said yes. And he laughed at me! I was devastated and went home crying. I felt so ashamed that I had even answered his question. Of course I believed in miracles, angels, and God. Didn't he?

On the outside, my bat mitzvah was a success. I had done what I had set out to do — I had learned to read and write in Hebrew. Unfortunately, I didn't achieve my main goal — getting in touch with God. I guess He wasn't in my temple either.

After my bat mitzvah classes, I stopped learning anything about Judaism for a long, long time. I do have one special Jewish memory, though. I remember my mother lighting candles late Friday afternoon before sunset. Her head covered, she brought in Shabbat with a beautiful prayer. Standing next to her, basking in the warmth of the candles, and watching my mother recite the prayer in Hebrew — these are some of my most beautiful memories.

In high school, I was very involved in theater productions, choral, and orchestra. Over the next five years, many friends passed away. Two young girlfriends in high school were killed by a drunk driver, another friend was murdered while hitchhiking during the summer of her junior year, another was strangled during my second year of college, another died of leukemia, another hit by a truck, and another was hit by a train while trying to save a woman's life as she lay unconscious on the tracks. They both died.

What was going on here? I wondered. What was life all about? What was dying all about?

I never imagined I would live past thirty, so I abandoned my search for truth and decided to live life to the fullest. I majored in photography and had a very successful career as a biomedical photographer. Working in the area of cancer research at three of the most prestigious universities and hospitals in the United States, I was involved in documenting radical surgeries and research. I was constantly faced with the delicate balance between life and death. Avoid them as I might try, all my questions resurfaced.

What was life all about? I wondered. Where could I find answers?

Not long after, I moved to the West Coast, and in three sequential moves, all my neighbors were Messianic Jews. I felt that God was sending me a sign.

My new neighbors weren't really Christians, I thought. They didn't celebrate Christian holidays like Christmas and Easter. They only celebrated the biblical holidays. They had Jewish names. They met on Saturday mornings for services, not Sundays. They believed in angels, miracles, and God. They quoted Scriptures from the Bible that they said proved that Jesus is the Messiah. One Saturday morning, I went to their Messianic congregation in town. They were praying and lifting their arms up to God. These were educated and sincere men, women, and children. Nice people, many of them Jewish. No crosses or pictures of Jesus, only a Star of David.

Well, I thought, *I'm home. I've finally found God.*

I was where I thought God wanted me to be. I could pray to God and believe in angels and still stay Jewish. I became a Messianic Jew, memorizing passages and eventually even doing some missionizing and recruiting.

Within a few years, though, I began to question the truth of the Messiahship of Jesus. It didn't happen overnight. I kept noticing hypocrisy in what I was seeing. They rejected the Jewish tradition, claiming that only the literal Bible was Divine. Yet they said blessings in Hebrew that didn't appear explicitly in the Bible at all, only in the Jewish tradition. The men would wear prayer shawls but not tefillin. Why one and not the other? They wore the tzitzit strings, but on their belt buckles, not on garments as the verse in the Bible clearly says to. They would quote passages out of context, twisting the meaning completely. When I would ask for explanations, they would move on to a different verse, claiming I had to have faith. I was told of several Messianic rabbis who were raised Orthodox, went to yeshivot, and had come to "see the light." If they were convinced of the authenticity of Jesus, I was told, why couldn't I be?

I tracked down these "rabbis" one by one, calling around the United States, Canada, Australia, and South Africa. Not one of them had had any serious Jewish education, or been raised Orthodox. Certainly none of them had been to a yeshivah. The deeper I dug, the greater the lies. I was upset, confused, unhappy, and lost. Where was I to go? What was really true?

About that time — thank God — my mother (who lived three thousand miles away) somehow found Rabbi Tovia Singer, director of Outreach Judaism. He was an antimissionary Orthodox rabbi who knew the New Testament inside and out. She wanted me to talk to him when I next visited New York.

Needless to say, I eagerly awaited my next trip. We met that evening and sat in my mother's living room for over five hours, going back and forth from Jewish to Christian Scriptures. He kept calling me *"rebbetzin."* What did he mean? I wondered. He said he was born with gefilte fish in his blood. He came from a family of rabbis from generations past. He was funny, friendly, and more knowledgeable than anyone I'd ever met. To this day we have a wonderful rabbi-student relationship. I remember saying that we both can't be right. He agreed. "This is serious stuff," he said. I knew I had to find out who was right. Over time Rabbi Singer encouraged me to go to Israel and learn about what I knew little about: Judaism.

Seven months after my initial meeting with Rabbi Singer, I left the Messianic congregation after eight years as a member. I didn't know who Jesus was, but was unable to stay there with my doubts about the movement's authenticity. It became clear to me that none of them actually knew anything about Judaism. How could they judge where Jesus fit in?

Everything I knew about Judaism was through a Christian prism, and I needed to learn how Jewish beliefs are different from Christian and Messianic Jewish beliefs. Over the next year and a half I went to nearby shuls for evening classes, but knew I needed even more immersion in Judaism.

With time, I saw the Jesus claim for what it was — a combination of lack of knowledge on the part of the believers and in some cases deception on the part of the leaders and institutions. There is much to explain, but, simply put, the reason why Jews in his time rejected Jesus as the Messiah is the same reason educated Jews do today. He doesn't fit the basic scriptural qualifications of being the Messiah — the leader of the Jewish people who will lead them to their land and their religion, ushering in an era of love, peace, and connection to God.* Clearly, neither the Messiah nor the Messianic age envisioned by the Bible and the Prophets have come.

But thankfully I learned much more about being Jewish than the reasons not to be Christian. I learned of how much God loves us, cares for us, and has not abandoned us. How He gave us a beautiful Torah to teach us how to get close to Him and how to achieve true happiness. How our people have spread the ideas of morality and goodness in the world and how we still have much

---

* For more information on why Jesus is not the Messiah, see Michael Skobac's essay in *Jewish Matters*.

to do. I learned what a great honor it is to be a Jew and what great role models we have in incredible Jewish women.

Now I live in Israel and visit the Western Wall whenever I can. I cried the first time I was there and still do sometimes when I go. It is there that I feel how close I have come to my grandparents, my heritage, and God.

I am sincerely grateful for all the steps I needed to take on my journey home. And now I have the opportunity to share what I have learned with many who are searching. And you, too, can help. Please show this essay to friends who are at risk — which includes almost anyone with a limited Jewish background. And most importantly, give your children (and yourselves) a serious Jewish education. In the long term, it is the only way Jews will stay Jewish.

> STEPHANIE lives in Israel with her husband. She has spoken to individuals and groups about her experiences and can be contacted via editor@jewishmatters.com. Rabbi Singer's Web site is www.outreachjudaism.org.

Dr. Elizabeth Kaufman

Women and Work

I suppose one of the biggest advantages of growing up with no religious background is never being aware of the common stereotype that Orthodox women are considered second-class citizens and that these poor unfortunate creatures are barefoot, always pregnant, and chained to the kitchen. After meeting Orthodox women of all stripes in Israel, I returned to New York only to be informed by my very Reform and less-than-Reform friends of the "actual" state of affairs. If I hadn't seen the reality for myself, I would have believed what they said and dismissed subsequent Jewish exposure as archaic and out of touch.

For those of us who question unproven stereotypes, let's get something perfectly clear: Jewish women work. And they have always worked, whether as shopkeepers, teachers, or professionals, whether in Babylon, European *shtetl*s, and twentieth-century America. And nowadays, like women all over the Western world, they work in every field. Some run their own businesses or are part of a larger corporation. Here in Israel one of my neighbors is a nuclear physicist. Another is a school principal. Several good friends are lawyers. One's a pediatrician. Two are successful artists. I'm a zoo veterinarian.

Many of these professional women have been religious since birth; equally as many are newly returned to

Orthodoxy. My point is, little is forbidden us. We work in the fields we want. We have open choices. We can choose to work part-time or full-time. We can choose to stay at home with our children, and no one will pooh-pooh us because this, too, is a valued choice.

Since I have always worked, perhaps I should tell my story. I first came into contact with traditional Judaism while working at the St. Louis Zoo as senior keeper of the Aquatic House. My brother introduced me to a college friend of his who'd just spent six months in a Jewish beginner's program in Israel. Nice guy. We got religious and we got married.

Actually, my return to Judaism took longer than that. My boyfriend wasn't doing anything Jewish when we met, but he talked about it. And kept on talking about it. I found it somewhat interesting but decided that it could never be relevant to me. Four months after we met, I moved to Colorado to start veterinary school. Three months after that we became engaged. Since my fiancé was determined to do this Judaism thing, we agreed to explore it in Israel before the wedding, and I agreed to keep an aborted form of Shabbat for the school year. That meant no school work on Saturdays and no telephone. Frankly, Shabbat saved my sanity that first grueling vet year.

Soon I realized — with Judaism increasingly, surprisingly relevant — that we needed to live near a Jewish community. I arranged a transfer to Tuft's Veterinary School for the following spring. We then flew to Israel to work out our various issues. At a women's yeshivah, I learned that my Shabbat observance wasn't even close to reality. Nevertheless, I'd fallen in love with the idea of Shabbat, the peace of mind it gave, and the increased energy and concentration it lent my week. My feminist mind liked Judaism's answers to women's issues.

My mother, upset at my new religious bent, predicted

that I was going to drop out of vet school, get married, get pregnant, and in twenty years get divorced with no way of supporting myself. The truth is, I did drop out of school and get married, and I did get pregnant right away. Mothers may always be right, but they're not always prophets: I graduated vet school, and I'm still married and still happy. And I can even support myself.

After our learning time in Israel, we moved to Boston and Tuft's. This was my first professional outing as an Orthodox woman. I was visibly pregnant with a scarf on my head. I was nervous about how people would accept me. But since vet school was what I had wanted my entire life, I plowed ahead. For six weeks no one spoke to me. Many years later, I learned that the vet students thought I was a medical student, the medical students thought I was a vet student, and everyone thought I was undergoing chemotherapy because of the scarf and wasn't that a shame because I was pregnant. It took a while to sort things out.

What surprised me most during my five years at Tuft's were the many people telling me how much they respected my melding of Jewish and professional life. Even the dean helped. When I told him, "I can't work or take exams on Sabbath or the holidays," he typed out, "Elizabeth Kaufman will be making requests for religious reasons. Please comply with everything she asks." He handed me the paper, saying, "Don't abuse this." To reciprocate, I worked every Sunday and all Christian, Greek, and Armenian holidays. I always tried to be polite and friendly. I always tried to behave better than I would have otherwise. Because, let's face it, I looked weird: the only one in a dress on night duty during large animal rotations, the only one pregnant with a scarf on her head.

By the time I left on aliyah, after a residency at Tuft's New England Wildlife Clinic, my colleagues threw me a party. They had done their research and were proud of the fact that it was a completely kosher affair. And because I ate Yodels constantly, they bought me a case for a going-away present. The truth is, Yodels were the only kosher snack in the vending machines, and I haven't eaten one since.

Time was forever tight. No time for phone calls, for correspondence, for errands. I was always racing home from classes to nurse the baby and see the husband, who did all the shopping, cooking, cleaning, and child care for five years. He insisted he wasn't a house husband and preferred to be called a housewife. I bought him flowers on Mother's Day.

Sixteen years later I'm working at four part-time jobs in two cities. I work for the Biblical Zoo and a private clinic. I teach at the Veterinary School of Hebrew University and teach pro bono for Jewish outreach programs throughout the country. I've found my present colleagues' responses akin to those of my student days — people go out of their way to accommodate my religious requirements and do so happily. I try to be cheerful and professional and religiously tolerant in return.

But priorities remain husband and kids. I'm always home by one, when my youngest child arrives. I reschedule my workweek if there's a school party or performance. No matter what work requires, my children come first. Because without a family-first priority solidly in place we cannot expect our own lives, or our children's, to be successful.

You might ask, if family is so important why should women work at all? The answer is different for everybody. For some it is an economic necessity; given a choice they would rather not work. For others, the challenges present in pursuing a professional career or any work outside the home adds a dimension that can help round us as balanced human beings. We can pursue interests and uncover potentials that homemaking and parenting, no matter how rewarding, leave unfulfilled for some women.

The Western world defines success as being at the top of one's field, wielding power and making lots of money. Being a housewife and mother, therefore, appears antithetical to accomplishment because one remains at home, not out making one's mark in the world. In stark contrast stands the Jewish definition of success: To what degree have you become a developed human being? How do you treat your spouse? Neighbors? Business partners? Are you honest with yourself? Are you emulating God's attributes? Are you raising children to do the same? Because, you see, in Judaism, building caring, principled people is an equally valued career for a woman — and a man.

Work and religious life are not mutually exclusive. Working can be an important part of a rich life. We merely need to decide which definition of success is most important to us so we can prioritize and organize our days, weeks, and months to give everything we can to those we care about, including ourselves. We need to decide how we wish to be affirmed in life, how we wish to be remembered after our deaths. Speaking for myself, I work because I am a better wife and mother for it, because my personality needs to have various intellectual interests and physical occupations outside the home. Work helps me appreciate more of what I've got.

DR. ELIZABETH KAUFMAN earned her doctorate of veterinary medicine from Tuft's University at Boston, Massachusetts. She has worked at several zoos in the United States and is currently staff veterinarian at the Tisch Family Zoological Gardens — the Biblical Zoo in Jerusalem. Dr. Kaufman also teaches at the Koret School of Veterinary Medicine of the Hebrew University at Beit Dagan and is a frequent lecturer on Jewish issues. She lives in Jerusalem with her husband and four awesome children.

Speaking about...
Gender and Roles

"Once I was at a rabbi's house for a Shabbat meal when he shocked me by announcing, 'In this family I make all the major decisions, and my wife makes all the minor decisions.' Needless to say, I was surprised. I'd seen the way he treats his wife and raises his kids. Had I been deceived? Was he really a chauvinist inside? Then the rabbi continued, 'I decide when the U.S. and Russia should go to war and what the economy is going to be like in ten years. She decides where we are going to live, who our friends are going to be, and where the kids are going to go to school.' There is a lot of wisdom in that one little joke if you think about it. I wish I had heard it thirty years ago." — Judy, 52

"I've been teaching Jewish women for many years, and I often find there is one block that keeps coming back. All the feminist issues make women feel as if they are disconnected from their heritage, that it has nothing to do with them as modern women. And so they become less involved, and their kids even less, and within a generation or two the family is no longer Jewish. It can leave so easily. And all of this is based on a great misunderstanding. Judaism's gender roles are empowering to women, not demeaning. All it takes is a little exposure to Torah in order to understand this." — Chana, 54

"I've never seen men respect their wives as much as in traditional Jewish homes." — Joanne, 24

"I think we've been misinformed. We're taught that a woman raising a family is tantamount to being a slave, something to be ashamed of. A hundred percent not true! It is the most important, responsible, beautiful, and creative role there is. Lots of people can fill my job, but only I can raise my child." — Stacy, 38

"I not only believe in gender differences, I celebrate them." — Donna, 45

Rebbetzin Feige Twerski

Progress

Compared with almost any era in history, women in our times have made significant inroads in the workplace. Although management analysts maintain that a "glass ceiling" still prevents women's access to the highest rungs of the corporate ladder, compensation and benefits levels for women vis-à-vis their male counterparts have been equalized to some degree. Furthermore, harassment litigation brought to national exposure within the last ten years has secured a safer, more respectful work environment for women.

We have become empowered and influential. We have become top executives, brilliant lawyers, respected doctors, and wealthy entrepreneurs. For the most part, I think we have successfully proven that, given the chance, we can "do a man's job."

Unfortunately, along with this gain has come a loss. This loss relates to the de-emphasis of the uniqueness of women. In order to properly put the matter in perspective, we must first appreciate that men and women are different.

In our world of mass production, there is a drive to standardize everything. This urgency to eliminate the unusual or the different has affected even our understanding of what it means to be human. Today, equality among human beings has somehow come to mean that everyone is the same. But, throughout our history, the Jewish people have maintained an unwavering and at times controversial stance: men and women are different. Our 3,500-year-old tradition maintains that the genders are parallel partners, unquestionably equal in importance, but definitely not the same.

Adam and Eve

My child once asked me, "When God created the world, why did God create men and women? Why not make just one kind?" It's a profound question. God is infinitely powerful and easily could have created a world populated by women only or a world of men only and fashioned a mechanism to have the one sex reproduce itself.

Instead, what did God do? "In the image of God He created him; male and female He created them" (Genesis 1:27).

In creating two distinct sexes, male and female, God was indicating there is a need for that which a male can contribute to the world and a need for a female's contribution to the world — and they are not the same thing. Everything in creation is necessary — nothing was created without a purpose. Therefore the existence of two sexes means we absolutely need the unique strengths of both.

Beautiful Balance

The male and female contribution goes beyond the human realm; we find that the entire world is a balance of male and female. Our mystical literature teaches us that the world was created through the letters of the Hebrew language, and that Hebrew words are not arbitrary symbols, but reflections of the inner reality of the entities they describe. In Hebrew, there is no "it." Every noun is either of male or female gender.

Take the Hebrew word for body, *guf. Guf* is a masculine term. Then you have the Hebrew word for soul, *neshamah. Neshamah* is feminine. In Jewish belief, the person is both *neshamah* and *guf.*

One might argue about which is more important, body or soul. Some might say the body. After all, that's the part of our being we relate to most directly; it's what we see. But what value is a body without a soul? It's like a garment without a person. Others might argue that the soul is more important, for at the deepest level, it is who we are. But what good is a soul if you don't have a body to put it in? The body is the tool with which we actualize the potential of the soul.

You have the same partnership in the Hebrew terms for tree and earth. *Etz,* "tree," is male. *Adamah*, "earth," is female. Without the earth, you could not have the tree, for it would not have a place from which to grow. Yet without the tree, the earth has not fulfilled its purpose. The earth sustains the tree, and the tree is an expression of the earth.

Within every human being, too, there are female and masculine properties. When we speak about the uniqueness of women or the uniqueness of men, we speak about the primary thrust of the human, but each gender includes the properties of the other. It makes sense that each human being has this balance of both masculine and feminine attributes because we are created in the image of God, and God has both masculine and feminine aspects.

This does not mean that God is a man or that God is a woman. We can't really say what God *is,* because God's essence is beyond human comprehension. When we say that God has both masculine and feminine properties, we are looking at the ways in which God's Presence manifests itself in the world. God acts in both masculine and feminine ways. Understanding these manifestations require an extensive background in Talmudic and mystical teachings. However, even those without this background can see hints of their existence in the Hebrew language itself: A common name for God in Hebrew literature is HaKadosh Baruch Hu, which means "the Holy One, blessed be He," a masculine construction in Hebrew grammar. But the Shechinah, God's Presence in this world, is a feminine construction.

Living in the Image of God

One of the responsibilities of our being made in the image of God is that we are supposed to act like God to the best of our abilities.

Men were given an extra share of the God-like masculine way of being. They are supposed to refine the masculine spiritual potential they have. Women were given an extra share of the God-like feminine way of being. Our task as women, then, is to refine the feminine spiritual ability we have and bring it to the highest expression we can in this world, within the particular life situations in which we're placed.

This is not a small task. Yet this very difficult assignment has become even harder today because women are convinced that the womanly side of them is something either to be ignored or, at best, relegated to an inferior role in their lives.

Unfortunately, our society has bought into the masculine way of being and devalued the feminine way of being — the special feminine contribution. Our success in the workplace has often led to us acting more like men. We think that in order to succeed we must act as aggressively as men, we must dress like men, and we must stifle everything feminine. "It's a man's world," we say, and the sad thing is, we believe it.

The tragic result is that a lot of really wonderful feminine properties are being lost along the way.

At a certain point in the 1960s, it became taboo to refer to the woman in conjunction with the home. Thankfully, we have recovered somewhat from the excesses of that period, and more women are realizing that raising a family is as honorable and important a job as paid work is outside the home, if not more so. Still society today usually sees the role of homemaker as secondary.

Our society has devalued the home and offers little or no support for the courageous woman who chooses the roles of wife and mother as her primary career. Nevertheless, I believe these women to be the unheralded heroes of our time. They are the ones who impact our lives in far deeper realms than do publicly renowned women.

These are the mothers, grandmothers, aunts, and teachers who notice us and go beyond themselves to show us care and concern. It is the memories of these women that fill us with warmth and solace in the cold winters and fragile moments of our lives.

For Jewish women, therefore, the question is not, are we able to be successful out there? By now it is clear that we can be. The real question is, should being successful out there be our major focus in life? When we look back at our lives, is that what we'll be most proud of?

I am not suggesting that women throw away successful careers and stay home exclusively. There is no obligation for women to stay home. And for many, economic situations required women to work outside the home.

At a deeper level, women must consider their need for personal fulfillment. The *Zohar*, the foremost kabbalistic work of our tradition, defines the commandment to "be fruitful and multiply" in Genesis 1:28 to include a wide spectrum of human creativity. Modern women especially often feel the need to be active outside the home.

However, the Torah emphasizes the importance of the home. It should not be neglected or made secondary. The single most important contribution most people will make to society is bringing up good children. There is a story of a rabbi speaking somewhere in the U.S., trying to explain to people how much happiness and meaning Judaism can add to their lives. A woman gets up and says, "That is very nice for you, Rabbi. You are studying and teaching. But where is your wife — in the kitchen cooking fish?" The rabbi answers, "I am proud to say that my wife is a professional woman, in charge of a facility for eight children. She is the director of the institution and is responsible for the children's physical, emotional, and spiritual needs." The audience applauds, and the woman who asked the question sits down, satisfied. Then the rabbi adds with a smile, "Actually, the institution is my home, and those eight children are my own."

This story describes a common attitude toward family. As long as a woman is caring for children in a professional mode, as director of a facility, it is all right and she is considered a success. But running a home is not enough — the woman is secondary and unimportant. In today's upside down world, it seems working with someone else's kids is worthy of more applause than working with one's own.

The Power of Being Who We Are

Throughout the ages, in history's glorious seasons and in times of persecution, trials, and travails, Jewish homes have served as an oasis, resistant and free of the raging storms plaguing civilization. Through it all, the Jewish people have survived because the women among them refused to compromise their values and roles in the face of the superficial and capricious fads of the societies in which they lived. As our oral tradition states, "Everything is determined by the woman." Throughout history, it has been women who have been the vigilant guardians of the Jewish home and thereby its values, morals, and ethics.

If we refuse to be ourselves, we stymie the very purpose of creation. God needs each one of us to do that which no one else can do — to perfect that share of the world that was given to us to perfect. It's only in being who we truly are that we can begin to accomplish these lofty goals. And only with the strengths of both the male and the female working together can we reach the ultimate perfection of the world.

Furthermore, if we deny our feminine sides, we will only damage ourselves. The heart of this idea may have best been expressed by the Kotzker Rebbe, an outstanding Jewish educator and philosopher of the nineteenth century. He said, "If I am I because I am I, and you are you because you are you, then I am I and you are you. But if I am I because you are you, and you are you because I am I, then you are not you and I am not I."

In other words, the only way that "I am I" is if I am true to myself — if I define myself according to what I know to be true and important. But if I define myself according to the predominant values of the society around me, then I am not being true to who I really am. And if the predominant value of the society is a masculine one, then I'm at risk of ignoring perhaps the most basic part of myself.

REBBETZIN FEIGE TWERSKI is a descendant of a noted Romanian chassidic family. She came to the United States as a young girl and grew up in Brooklyn, New York. She has written for a wide spectrum of Jewish journals worldwide and is a much sought after speaker on a myriad of Judaic subjects. She and her husband, Rabbi Michel Twerski, founded the Torah Foundation of Milwaukee, an educational center that reaches out to Jews of all backgrounds.

Sonya Jazen and Stephanie Porter

Three Misconceptions about Jewish Marriage

Men "buy" their wives at the traditional Jewish wedding ceremony.

Untrue. Jewish women are not "owned" by their husbands. We are full and equal partners in marriage. A man marries a woman through giving her something of value, usually a ring. She does not present anything to him because her agreement is clear by her acceptance of the ring. This aspect of the wedding ceremony is in line with Jewish contract law, in which one party is active while the other is passive. In this case, the man is the active partner because most often he is the one who actively courts his wife.

The Jewish marriage contract is anti-woman.

I assume that you are referring to the *ketubah*, which is the traditional Jewish marriage contract. Before we directly refer to the issue at hand, we should state clearly that classical Judaism definitely believes in love and romance within marriage. The mikveh cycle has as one of its many benefits the maintenance of that special, exciting feeling throughout married life.

Yet having a legal contract is very important. It provides the security and the clarity of obligations that put a woman's mind at ease and let her enjoy that romantic feeling without having to worry. It outlines explicitly the husband's main obligations to his wife — providing food, clothing, and intimacy. It also outlines exactly how much money he is obligated to give her in the case of divorce (sometimes a pretty hefty sum). In this sense, the *ketubah* is basically a prenuptial agreement that has been in use for millennia. In fact, *ketubot* are so central to marriage that Jewish grooms have been handing their brides beautifully decorated ones since at least medieval times (see the *Encyclopedia Judaica* for beautiful examples). In our day, many women hang these beautiful *ketubot* up on the walls of their homes.

Women do all the housework.

Actually, Jewish law states clearly that if the couple can afford it they must hire help, and a husband can be forced to pay if he is hesitant. When financial realities do not allow hiring help, the woman only does the housework if they together agree to a relationship in which the husband is responsible for bringing home all of the family's income while the wife alone runs the home. Even in that case, husbands should try to help — and usually they do.

A couple is allowed to choose a different relationship if they prefer (for example, job sharing or even her working and him not). Traditionally, since many women want to raise the children themselves, they run the home and the husbands work outside to bring in the income. Consequently, most (not all!) of the household chores fall on these women. Today, in many religious communities, often out of economic necessity, many couples choose for the wife to work at least part-time outside the home, and the husband therefore takes on a bigger share of the burden.

Whoever does it, though, housework should not be

relished. More recently, students of the famed Kelm Yeshivah vied for the privilege of emptying the garbage. The home, the study hall, and the Temple are all holy places, and keeping them clean is an important function in maintaining their holiness.

SONYA JAZEN wishes to thank the people at www.heritageretreats.org for providing wonderful summer seminars for young Jewish women.

STEPHANIE PORTER has been involved with NCSY (National Conference of Synagogue Youth), which she wishes to thank for giving her such a strong Jewish identity during her teenage years.

Meira Svirsky

Women and Minyan

Why can't women be counted in a minyan, the traditional quorum of ten men required before reciting certain prayers?

This is a question I often hear when teaching classes on women and Judaism. To answer it, we must first explore the origins of communal prayer — its purpose and its relevance to women.

The Torah given to the Jewish people on Mount Sinai made no mention of a synagogue and gave no mitzvah of public prayer. On the contrary, our matriarchs and patriarchs — the spiritual archetypes and role models of the Jewish people — not only prayed individually but accomplished great things by doing so.

So what brought about the change? How did Judaism evolve to incorporate the notion of synagogue, communal prayer, and minyan?

The concept of communal prayer began as a Rabbinic edict derived from the incident in the Torah involving the spies sent to the Land of Israel after the Jewish people left Egypt. While in the desert, all of our physical needs were taken care of, leaving each individual free to pursue and master the newly given Torah accepted at Mount Sinai. God had assured the people that when it was time they would enter the land without any problems.

Still, there were certain elements among the Jewish people who not only lacked trust in God, but were also resistant to leaving this "good life" in the desert. It was from this group that the idea came to send spies to scope out the land — possibly as a delay tactic or even part of a strategy to avoid leaving the desert altogether.

This group came to Moses with their plan. After consulting with God, Moses decided to try a bit of reverse psychology. "Go ahead," Moses said to them, hoping his confidence that the spies would come back with positive findings would discourage them from making the trip altogether.

Moses' strategy, unfortunately, proved ineffective. Twelve spies — one from each tribe — were sent to the land; ten came back with an evil report. All the men (save a few) believed the report and, despairing of their imagined fate, lamented having to enter the land. As a result, all of these men were denied entry into the Land of Israel and were decreed to die in the desert.

From this incident — where ten men had convened for evil purposes and had desecrated God's Name — a mechanism was put in place for ten men to come together for positive purposes, namely, prayer, a means of sanctifying God's Name. To assure participation in such a congregation, certain prayers were forbidden to be said outside such a group.

Let's look at the women in the desert for a minute. None of the women believed the report of the spies. On the contrary, they remained steadfast in their trust in God and eager to enter the land as soon as the word was given. As such, they were not included in this new requirement, which was obviously a rectification for a deficiency found in the men. As always, women remained capable of accessing holiness as individuals and through praying as individuals.

Contrary to a popular misconception, we see that it

is not because of some superior spiritual standing that only men are counted in a minyan, the quorum necessary for communal prayer. Quite the opposite.

Perhaps the following story gives a humorous insight as to why men are required to pray in a minyan and women are not.

A rabbi I know once taught a class in which a priest was one of his students. The question of minyan vis-à-vis women was raised and explained this way. At this point, the priest raised his hand to speak.

"You Jews are brilliant!" he exclaimed. "Every Sunday in my church the pews are filled with women. I've tried everything to get the men to come as well. If we had this concept of minyan, things would be different."

Simply put, men need the minyan, while women don't.

In our modern world, most Jews are not aware of many of the 613 Torah commandments required of us. At the same time, involvement in a synagogue has taken on enormous proportions never intended by those who originated the institution of communal prayer. While it is true that synagogue participation in our time has served to maintain a Jewish identity for those otherwise distant from their Jewish heritage, we must be honest enough to acknowledge that the synagogue is and always was intended to be only a small part of Judaism aimed at correcting a deficiency in part of the population. Moreover, for a synagogue to effectively correct this deficiency, its focus must be on communal prayer, not social activities.

All said, no one would deny the merit of women attending and participating in services at a synagogue to enhance their own spirituality. However, it's important to understand how Jewish law works in the case of a voluntary mitzvah.

Jewish law states that one who is not obligated in a

given mitzvah cannot perform the mitzvah for one who is. Moreover, in Jewish law, one who is not obligated in a certain mitzvah also does not have the option — in many cases — of opting into it even if he so desires. Let's see how this works on a practical level.

If you are planning to eat bread, for example, you are obligated to say the appropriate blessing. If others are eating bread with you, you may include them in your blessing (this is done simply through your intention to do so), and through you they also will have fulfilled their obligation. However, if you are not eating bread, you cannot discharge their obligation to make a blessing by doing it for them.

Let's take another example, of a man who has lost a member of his immediate family member. Before the burial, this man, referred to as an *onen*, is not obligated in any positive commandments, of which prayer is an example. Since he is not obligated in this mitzvah, he may not be counted as one of the ten males required for a minyan.

Similarly, a woman, for the reasons mentioned above, is not obligated in the mitzvah of communal prayer. Therefore, she cannot discharge this mitzvah for someone who is obligated, meaning she cannot be counted as one of the ten men required for a minyan. Not a value judgment, rather a technical point of Jewish law.

MEIRA SVIRSKY earned her master's degree in philosophy from the University of Texas at Austin. She worked as a professional journalist in Texas for ten years. Presently, she teaches at JEWEL (the Jewish Women's Education League, an introductory program for educated women interested in their Jewish heritage, located in Jerusalem), among other programs. She is coauthor with Rabbi Yitzhak Berkowitz of a soon-to-be-published book on the laws and philosophy of Jewish marriage and sexuality. She is married, has four children, and lives in the Old City of Jerusalem.

Editors' note: This explanation is found in Lisa Aiken's *To Be a Jewish Woman*, page 98. Rabbi Mordechai Tendler cautions that a full understanding of this concept depends on a broad knowledge of kabbalah and the idea of *tikkun*. On a simple level, he explains, since women were not involved in the mistake, at a mystical level they are not held responsible for the repair.

Speaking about...
Biblical Texts

"At a superficial glance, women are secondary in the Jewish tradition, but how often are superficial glances accurate? In reality, the woman's sphere is not inferior at all. It is a community of meaning and action. We don't compete with another's attention. We really like one another, and we are so, so important." — Lea, 30

"Women transmit culture and values. We are the guardians of a family's moral standards and sensitivities." — Rachel, 31

"I was told recently about some radical Jewish feminists who made a circumcision ceremony for an eight-day-old Jewish baby. It had all the trappings of a traditional bris, with one major exception — the baby was a girl! These well-intentioned ladies were trying to express themselves religiously as Jewish women and ended up doing the opposite: they basically admitted that men continue to serve as their role models. Why do we have to do what men do to feel equal? If these unfortunate women knew more about the richness of Jewish womanhood, they would not have to copy men's activities in order to feel worthy." — Rina, 36

"I like the fact that men and women have different paths to holiness. We complement each other: we are separate, unique, yet together. The world needs us women and our unique view of things. Men have a few extra time-bound mitzvot, such as tallit and tefillin, because they need the spiritual discipline. We don't. We have our own ways of connecting to spirituality." — Elaine, 65

Sara Esther Crispe

Mother of All Life

The Torah calls the first woman in the history of creation Chavah, Eve in English. The English name Eve is related etymologically to the word *evil*. Non-Jewish sources so named her because she was the first being to sin, bringing death and darkness into the world (our tradition sees the issue as quite complex, and it is often regarded as a descent for the sake of an ascent). The English name Eve not only lacks the meaning inherent in the biblical name Chavah, but is fundamentally opposed to what the word *chavah* means, who she was, and what she represents.

According to the Jewish mystical tradition, there are three main concepts connected to the Hebrew name Chavah. The first comes from the explanation given in the Torah itself: because she is *"em kol chai* — the mother of all life" (Genesis 3:20).

The medieval commentator Rashi explains this phrase. The name Chavah is a derivative of the Hebrew word *chayah*, meaning "living one." Chavah embodies both the essence of life itself and the creative ability to grant that life to others. The concept "mother of all life" expresses not only the ability to physically give birth, but also to create, nourish, and enhance all facets of life. This is the ability of a mother — to take something from the state of potential, develop it, and bring it to actualization through her creative abilities.

The second understanding of the name Chavah focuses on its connection to the word *chavayah*, which means "experience." Chavah is not only the mother of life but also represents the experience of life.

With this explanation, we can better understand the relationship between her and Adam, her husband. The name Adam is not only a first name whose literal meaning is "man," but also refers to mankind, to humanity in general. Therefore, Adam-humanity is married to Chavah-experience, representing the totality of human experience, the human condition.

The third meaning stems from a verse in the book of Psalms (19:3) which reads, "Night following night expresses knowledge." The Hebrew word for "expression" is *yechaveh*, which is also related to the word *chavah*. In this vein, there is a verse in the book of Job (36:2) which states, "Wait for me a little while, and I will show you." The Hebrew phrase for "I will show you" is *ve'achavecha*, again from the same root. This third meaning of Chavah can be understood as "expression," "revelation," or "manifestation."

Ultimately, these three meanings work together. How does Chavah, the first woman, represent the mother of all life? Through experience as expression and through expression as experience she mothers all life. She shapes and develops formless matter, carrying it within her until it is ready to be born. However, the mothering process does not end with physical birth, for she then continues to nurse this life, feeding and sustaining it physically, emotionally, and spiritually. She continues to nourish it throughout its life, helping to actualize its latent potential and helping this life to develop and experience its utmost expression. And by doing this, she will constantly be giving birth to new levels of ability and depth of life experience, both within herself and within all those around her, earning the title "mother of all life."

SARA ESTHER CRISPE is the associate director of Torat Chesed—The Jerusalem Torah Institute for Women, an institute for intensive learning of Jewish mysticism and Chassidut through a focus on creative expression and individual growth. She is also on the team of writers for the Gal Einai Institute, an organization for disseminating the teachings of Rabbi Yitzchak Ginsburgh, renowned master of the Jewish esoteric tradition.

Dr. Esther Shkop

Visions of the Divine: Gender in Textual Imagery

M uch has been made of male dominance in Judaism which, it is argued, is rooted in the biblical and liturgical conception of God in masculine images. Indeed, when Jewish sources wish to represent God as the ultimate force, that power is represented in the metaphor of *Gibor*, Hero, and *Ish milchamah*, Man of war. When the representation is meant to indicate that God is the source of righteous judgment, He is depicted as a *shofet*, the masculine word for judge; when as a benign yet stern father, God is described as *Avinu shebaShamayim*, our Father in Heaven. These images are undoubtedly masculine. And they are meant to be.

However, in essence, God is neither feminine nor masculine. God's essence is indescribable in any human terms, as Maimonides's fourth principle of faith states: "The Creator...is not physical and is not affected by physical phenomena" (commentary to the Mishnah, *Sanhedrin*, ch. 10). The descriptive references, then, are for our benefit, to allow us to relate to the Divine. Undoubtedly women can and should relate to God as envisaged in masculine imagery. However, if the imagery used in Judaic texts were solely masculine, one might be led to believe that there is a uniquely masculine approach to Judaism's conception of God. Judaic theology would thus foster a closer affinity with the world of men than that of women. Indeed, some contemporary women feel disconnected from their heritage, convinced that it simply does not speak to them as women.

In truth, masculine imagery represents only one portion of references to God in Jewish texts. The Tanach (the five books of the Bible and the Prophets and Writings) is, in fact, replete with feminine imagery.

The Image of God

The Torah relates that God created the first being, Adam, "in His image, in the image of God He created him; male and female He created them" (Genesis 1:27). The great commentator known as the Malbim (in his work *Ayelet HaShachar*, ch. 31) states that wherever the concept of Adam is used in biblical and Talmudic writings, it denotes both male and female. In other words, when God first created Adam — the first being created in the image of God — he was formed with both female and male aspects, as an androgynous being. Only later does the Bible describe the separation of the male and female in the formation of Adam and Eve. Henceforth, the Divine image is as intrinsic in the woman as it is in the man, and, indeed, in the absence of either man or woman, there is no complete image of God.

E-l Rachum, Merciful God

When describing the unconditional love that cannot — and will not — be extinguished by betrayal and abandonment, Moses evokes the image of maternal compassion with the description of God as *E-l Rachum*, the Merciful God, "Who will not fail you, nor destroy you" (Deuteronomy 4:31). The great nineteenth-century commentator Rabbi Samson Raphael Hirsch illuminated the fact that the concept of *rachum*, mercy, is rooted in the noun *rechem*, which means "womb." The Jewish conception of compassion and love is grounded in the essentially feminine image of the womb, which holds, nurtures, and protects the fetus — be it perfect or malformed, pretty or ugly, worthy or undeserving.

Inspired by the words of the Torah, the prophet Isaiah adds more drama and depth to the maternal imagery. He renders God as the loving Mother of Israel who can never forget the child She bore and suckled, who then asks incredulously, "Can a woman forget her babe, cease loving the son of her belly? Indeed, these may forget, but I will never forget you" (Isaiah 49:15).

In a similar vein, Isaiah presents God as the Source of life and peace. With a descriptive personification of a nursing mother, he portrays the great metaphor of God's comfort:

> I stretch out to her like a river of peace, like a stream flowing with the honor of the nations, and you may suckle. You will be carried on the side and played with on the knees. As one whose mother comforts him, so I will comfort you; and you will be comforted in Jerusalem.
>
> (Isaiah 66:12–13)

Often in his prophecies of comfort, Isaiah presents God in woman-to-woman dialogue with the collective of Israel, Zion, who is complaining about her long years of suffering. God soothes the despairing Zion like a sympathetic midwife, explaining that her pains are but the travails that precede birth and asking rhetorically, "Will I bring you to the breaking point and not bring forth? If I am the deliverer [midwife], will I stop [the birth]...?" (Isaiah 66:9).

Similarly, the maternal imagery of God can be found throughout Psalms, the primary source of Jewish liturgy. This is quite explicit in chapter 22 (written by King David about four centuries before Isaiah), in which the poetry transposes the babe's reliance on the mother's breast with its reliance on God:

> For You are the One Who drew me out of the belly, the One Who secured me on my mother's breasts. Upon You I have been cast from the womb; from my mother's belly You have been my God.
>
> (Psalms 22:10–11)

This image of God's relation to the Jewish people as that of the nonjudgmental, unconditionally loving Mother flowers in the poetic renditions of the later Prophets. In his description of the exodus from Egypt and the birth of Israel as a nation, Ezekiel employs the concept of God as a high-soaring eagle who takes note of Israel, depicted as an unwanted, abandoned female infant wallowing in blood (Ezekiel 16:6). The hovering Presence, resolute that the infant will live, is contrasted to the parents and midwives who had rejected her. While they had cast her off, still attached to the afterbirth, God embraces, washes, and swaddles the baby girl.

The warmth with which Ezekiel describes the dressing and adorning of the growing babe sheds a new and warm light on the rituals with which mothers bestow gentle affection on their children. There is no more intimate and tender act of giving than that of a woman when she cleanses her baby and dresses it in pretty clothes. To be able to adore a baby despite its filth, to coo and sweet-talk a child while wiping its bottom, to wash and anoint its skin, and then cover it with embroidered swaddling probably does more for building a

child's self-esteem than we can ever know. That God as-
cribes to "Himself" such loving, albeit mundane acts
speaks more to the value of what has been called
"women's work" than all the exhortations of modern
literature.

Imagery of Female Strength

Lest it seem that the use of the feminine metaphor is
limited to depictions of nurturing and tender motherhood, Isaiah confounds our prejudices. Not only does
the woman personify the collective of the Jewish people
in its relation to God, but the prophet directly envisions
God as a woman of strength.

Isaiah describes, in the third person, the vengeance
of God against our enemies:

> As a mighty man He will go out; like a man of
> war He will stir up jealousy. He will blare, even
> scream, as He overcomes His enemies.
>
> (Isaiah 42:13)

However, in the development of that same pro-
phetic vision, the voice moves to the first person, as God
speaks of long-simmering fury. The *Ish milchamah*, the
Man of war, undergoes a metamorphosis and emerges
in the strength and cries of a birthing woman in the
throes of labor:

> I have forever held my peace, I have hushed and
> refrained Myself; now, like a birthing woman, I
> will cry out, panting and gasping at once.
>
> (Isaiah 42:14)

The Malbim, in his commentary on this verse,
differentiates between the words *eshom*, rapid, panting
exhalations, and *eshaf*, which refers to gasping inhala-
tions. In what might be the first description of the
Lamaze method, the prophet transforms the allegorical

meaning inherent in the image of the birthing woman. She is no longer seen as a victim of forces she cannot control; instead, she is rendered as the symbol of strength, of creative force. Interestingly, the Hebrew word *chayil*, "valor" or "force," which connotes labor contractions, is the root of the Hebrew words for military forces and soldier.

The Divine Name

In English translations of Judaic texts, the Divinity is referred to as God, Lord, or Hashem (literally, "the Name"). Yet God has a Name, the famous tetragrammaton, the four-lettered Name of Hashem, which is made up of the letters *yud-heh* and *vav-heh*. This ineffable Name of Hashem is a contraction of the Hebrew verb *to be* in the past, present, and future, denoting God's existence before time, in the present, and after the end of time, and is therefore often translated as "the Eternal." In the Hebraic source, this Name is written as a feminine noun and signifies the aspect of *rachamim*, mercy, which, as indicated above, is quintessentially feminine. Thus every blessing and prayer we say, every evocation of the Eternal Presence, kabbalistically called the "Shechinah," is in fact an evocation of the feminine concept — the unconditional love of the Creator.

Moreover, this feminine four-lettered Name of Hashem is used throughout the Torah and all of our liturgy to suggest *hashgachah pratit*. *Hashgachah pratit*, commonly translated in English as "Divine providence," follows each person like a shadow, protecting and guiding each human being and according infinite value to each individual. Its presence is invisible, but it is the One with which we commune, for it is with us at all times. This concept is unlike the concept of Elokim, another of God's Names, which is written as a plural masculine noun and signifies the forces and multiple powers manifest in nature — visible yet uncontrollable, relentless, and impersonal.

One can only be impressed by the majestic beauty and profound emotion that Jewish sources, especially the Prophets, conjure through the use of feminine imagery. The numerous and various strong feminine images more than balance out the masculine ones. While we must remember that the Divine is beyond form and gender, human language by necessity conceives even the most abstract in visual images. The multiplicity of feminine images alongside the masculine, and the context in which one or the other is used, requires close study and often mystical understanding.

Careful analysis of the Hebraic texts will reveal that religious experiences and the immediacy of God are to be found in the world of women no less than in that of men. It would be a tragedy — and a travesty — to "castrate" the language, for it would then remove God from the experiential milieus of both men and women, rendering us mortals mute, unable to commune with or communicate about our Creator.

DR. ESTHER SHKOP is dean of the Anne Blitstein Teachers Institute for women of Hebrew Theological College and is associate professor of Bible. A tenth-generation sabra with a legacy of a Rabbinic family renowned in Old Jerusalem, Dr. Shkop was educated in Israel and the United States.

Lori Palatnik

Who We Are,
Where We Are Going

I used to help people make their kitchens kosher. Once I was pulling pots and pans out of a woman's cupboard when she sighed heavily. "Lori," she said, "going kosher, maybe, but there are a lot of things about this religion that bother me, primarily the role of women. Let's face it. Judaism is all about men, the Torah is about men, and I can't stand it."

I stopped pulling out the pots and pans. "Have you ever read the Torah?" I asked.

"Well, when I was a kid we must have read some of it in Hebrew school...."

"If you read the Torah," I continued, "you'll notice that not only are there a lot of women in it, but also that it's the women who save the Jewish people time and time again."

She looked surprised and skeptical. I closed the cupboards. The kitchen could wait, I figured. It was time to open up the Five Books. There were so many examples of the greatness of women in the Torah that it was hard to decide where to start. I chose a story that is familiar to us all (thanks to Cecil B. DeMille's movie), the story of the Jewish people leaving Egypt.

The Torah recounts that after being enslaved for

hundreds of years, the Jewish people were finally allowed to go free. This, the Talmud says, was in the merit of Jewish women. What did they do that was so meritorious?

Not Giving Up

Pharaoh had fortunetellers who could see into the future. They told him that a baby boy (we know him as Moses) would be born to the Hebrews who would grow up and lead them out of Egypt. Pharaoh liked having millions of slaves and obviously did not want them to leave. He decreed that all Jewish newborn boys would be killed.[1]

What was the reaction of the Jewish men? Amram, a great sage and scholar, was the leader of the Jewish people at the time (and the father-to-be of Moses). He concluded that the men should separate and divorce their wives, for how can one have children knowing they will be murdered? The men followed his lead.[2] In the end, his daughter, Miriam, a great prophetess, convinced her father otherwise, for Pharaoh had acted only against the boys, while Amram's decision was against both boys and girls.

How did the women react during the enslavement? They used their copper mirrors to beautify themselves and went to be with their husbands in the fields.[3] They knew that this was not the time to give up. God had promised that the Jewish people would survive. He would save us. The women knew that if the Jewish people stopped having children Pharaoh would win.

But how do we know that their motivations were pure?

Fast forward now to the place where God instructs the Jewish people to build a Tabernacle in the desert that the Jewish people would carry as they encamped. It would house the tablets on which were engraved the Ten Commandments and would be a place where God's Presence would dwell.

A central part of the Tabernacle would be the washbasin where the *kohanim*, the priests, would wash before performing the Divine service:

> God spoke to Moses saying: "Make a copper washbasin along with a copper base for it. Place it between the altar and the Communion Tent and fill it with water for washing."
>
> (Exodus 30:17–18)

Where did the copper come from to fashion the washbasin? Our tradition says it was made from the copper mirrors of the women. Knowing that the mirrors were previously used for romance, Moses was hesitant to use them for such a holy purpose. God admonished him, "Accept them. These mirrors are most beloved to Me."[4]

Clearly the intention of the Jewish women was pure. "Don't give up" was their message to their men. "The Jewish people will go on. God will indeed redeem us."

Trust in the Future

So the Jewish people flee from Egypt. At one point it looked like it was all going to end — the sea was in front of them; the Egyptians were coming up fast behind them. What were they to do? Four options were suggested: to give up and go back to Egypt to be slaves once again, to fight to the finish and take some Egyptians with them in death, to throw themselves into the sea and commit suicide, or to cry out in anguish. All these responses, however, showed a lack of trust in God's ability to save them. It took Nachshon ben Aminadav to enter the water first, demonstrating his great trust in the God Who had just performed miracles for them. With his heroic entry, God split the sea, and all twelve tribes passed through safely.

Interesting is the women's attitude throughout these events — like Nachshon, they did not show a lack of trust. How do we know this? After the sea splits and the Jewish people are safe on the other side, they look back and see the sea engulfing the Egyptians.

> Miriam the prophetess, Aaron's sister, took the drum in her hand, and all the women followed her with musical instruments and dancing. Miriam led them in the response "Sing to God for His great victory; horse and rider He cast into the sea."
>
> (Exodus 15:20–21)

At this point we have a question: Where did they get the musical instruments? In Egypt they were fleeing for their lives; in fact, they didn't even have time for the bread to rise! (We know this from our obligation to eat matzah at the Pesach seder in commemoration of their quick departure.) So how did they have time to pack musical instruments?[5]

Now, if you are neurotic like me and lie in bed at night worrying about everything under the sun, you may have had this thought: If, God forbid, your house were on fire and everyone was safely out of the house and you had time to grab one physical possession, what would it be? Most people say their photo albums. I, on the other hand, have loose photos in a million drawers and would die trying to retrieve them all. I would probably grab my beautiful, framed *ketubah* (marriage contract) off the wall and run.

The Jewish women had moments to grab one or two physical possessions, and what did they bring? Their drums and tambourines. Why? The women knew that there would come a time to dance and sing in praise of God. Thus, when things looked their worst, the women showed exemplary patience. They knew salvation would come. The same God who had brought the plagues would surely save them.

Keeping Clear

The story continues. They make it to Mount Sinai, where God reveals Himself to the entire Jewish people and begins to give the commandments. The whole thing is too much to handle, so the people ask Moses to go up the mountain and get the rest of the Torah himself and bring it down to them. He agrees and says he will be back in forty days. The Jews miscount and think he didn't return on time, fearing he is dead. The result? Some of them panic and create a golden calf.

Being in the desert, where did they get the gold to build this idol? The Torah says that the men involved had to "take the rings off the ears of their wives."[6] Clearly the women did not want to give up their jewelry. (In the movie the women were gaily throwing their bracelets and rings into the fire — read the Book; it's always better than the movie.)

But again, how do we know their motivations were pure? Perhaps they were materialistic women who wanted to keep their jewelry?

The proof is that later, when gold was needed for the building of the Tabernacle, the women were the first ones to come forward and give of their jewelry.[7] For a holy purpose, here is my jewelry; for an unholy purpose, you will have to rip it from my ears.

Ladies First

Moses returns to Mount Sinai to receive the second set of tablets. Before Moses descends, God tells him: "This is what you must say to the House of Jacob and tell the children of Israel...."[8]

All the commentators zero in on this line and point

out that the "House of Jacob" — *Beit Yaakov* — refers to
the Jewish women, and "the children of Israel," the
men.[9] Here God was instructing Moses to give the Torah
to the women first and then to the men. Why?

Suppose He gave it to the men first and they accepted the Torah: "Great Torah, business ethics, wisdom, depth — fine, we'll take it." And then it was
offered to the women. Imagine that they took a look
and said, "Hmmm, looks like a lot of work on Fridays to
me. No thanks." Would the Torah have survived even
one week? Not a chance.

Different scenario: The Torah is offered to the men,
and they see things like the prohibition against adultery
in it. "No thanks, we'll pass." And then it is offered to
the women. "Family, ethics, morality. Beautiful. We'll
take it."

Would the Torah live on? You bet it would. As contemporary psychologists agree (for example, Dr. John
Grey in *Men Are from Mars and Women Are from Venus*),
women are better at communication and interpersonal
relationships than men and are able to motivate the
people around them and inspire them to greatness.
Men, in general, are just not as skilled when it comes to
these matters.

The point is that the men's acceptance wouldn't
guarantee anything. Nor would their rejection. God
therefore told Moses to give the Torah to the Jewish
women first. If they accept it, it doesn't matter what the
men say; it will live for eternity.

We see this influential power of women in many
instances. The Talmud tells a story of a righteous
woman and a righteous man who marry. They are unable to have children so they mutually agree to divorce.
The righteous woman marries a man who is not so righteous and makes him righteous. The righteous man
marries a woman who is not so righteous, and he be-

comes not so righteous.

This story illustrates the power of the Jewish woman. She has the ability to impact on others on the deepest level. It is a gift that can be used — or abused.

Staying Loyal

Let us go on. The Jewish people continue on their journey through the desert. You would think we would be as happy as can be, protected by the Clouds of Glory, a well of water accompanying us, manna falling from the heavens. How grateful we must have been to Moses.

Well, not exactly...

A small but vocal group of men decided to question the leadership of Moses. Who appointed him anyway? (Well, actually, God did.) A rebellion was planned, led by Korach:

> Korach the son of Yitzhar began a rebellion along with Dathan and Aviram and On the son of Peleth....
>
> (Numbers 16:1)

Moses, the greatest and most effective leader in history, tries to reason with them, but they are not to be dissuaded. They convince others to join them. When they come to take over and give their own offerings to God as the new leaders, Moses goes specifically to Dathan and Aviram to try to reason with them. This is what happens:

> Moses had hardly finished speaking when the ground under them split. The earth opened its mouth and swallowed them and their houses, along with all the men who were with Korach and their property. They fell into the depths along with all that was theirs. The earth then covered them, and they were lost to the community.
>
> (Numbers 16:31–33)

This got everyone's attention.

But when you are learning Torah, there is one thing you must always keep in mind. There are no superfluous words. Every word, every letter, is there for a reason. If something is repeated, there is a reason. If something is left out, there is a reason. It should get your attention and spark questions.

And our question here is, what happened to On (pronounced *own*) the son of Peleth? He was specifically mentioned in the beginning of the rebellion, but when everyone was swallowed up, he was not present at all.

To fill in the gaps we must look to the Midrash, accounts from our oral tradition.

The Midrash[10] on these verses explains that On had a wife who got wind of his plans to join Korach in the rebellion. She tried to reason with him. How could he rebel against Moses after everything he had done? On, of course, did not listen and told her that the rebellion was planned for the next morning.

So that night she got him drunk. When Korach and his men came the next morning to fetch him, On's wife went to the entrance (inside, On lay in a stupor), uncovered her hair, and began to brush it.

Now, even though Korach and his followers were making a grave mistake, they were still very religious Jews. They were shocked to see a married woman with her hair uncovered. Embarrassed, they quickly bypassed the tent and went to the rebellion without him. Later, when On awoke, his wife explained what had occurred and how he was saved from death. (And I personally hope she reminded him of it every day for the rest of his life.)

This Land Is My Land

At last the Jewish people come to their destiny, to the border of the Land of Israel. Filled with fear, they hesitate to enter and instead send in twelve men to spy out the land. When they return, ten out of the twelve give a bad report, adding to their fears. The people refuse to enter. God punishes them by making them wander for forty years in order to enable that generation to die out. But this punishment was only directed at the men. The Jewish women did not participate in the sin of the spies. They were ready to enter and fulfill the destiny of the Jewish people as God had promised.

Indeed, of the original people who left Egypt, with the exception of Joshua and Caleb (the ones who gave a good report), only the women merited to go into the Land of Israel.

Woman's Legacy

What is the greatness of the Jewish woman? It is her trust in God. And this holds true today as it did then. Even in the face of adversity, she remains steadfast in her knowledge that the Almighty loves us and will see us through. She is an example to all those around her, striving for greatness and imbuing others with greatness.

It is our legacy. It is our sacred trust. May we merit to be a strong link in the chain of great Jewish women and may we empower our daughters and their daughters to continue this legacy forever.

A biography of the author can be found on page 99.

References

1. *Rashi* on Exodus 1:16.
2. *Talmud Bavli, Sotah* 12b.
3. *Rashi* on Exodus 38:8.
4. Ibid.
5. *Rashi* on Exodus 15:20.
6. Exodus 32:2.
7. Ibid. 35:22.

8. Ibid. 19:3.
9. *Rashi* on Exodus 19:3.
10. *Bemidbar Rabbah* 18:20.

Esther Wein

Binah: A Woman's Power

The Talmud comments (on Genesis 2:22) that women possess a certain power that, when properly cultivated, exceeds its counterpart in men. This intellectual power is called "*binah*," a word derived from the Hebrew root *bein*, which means "between." *Binah* is the ability to analyze and then distinguish between situations or entities that on the surface seem similar but are really quite different.

The definition of *binah* is found in one of the blessings said every morning: "You have given the rooster *binah* to distinguish between night and day." When the rooster crows, it still looks like night outside, but in fact it is the beginning of morning. The rooster's ability to know a situation, not for how it looks on the surface but for what it truly is, exemplifies *binah*.

The biblical matriarchs used the attribute of *binah* to create the Jewish people. Early in the book of Genesis, we read about Sarah, age ninety, and Abraham, age ninety-nine, who have devoted their lives to spreading novel, monotheistic ideas to a world steeped in idol worship. The couple is childless, and Sarah encourages Abraham to take a second wife, their maidservant Hagar, so that there will be another generation to continue their important work. Hagar gives birth to a son, Ishmael. In the meantime, God allows Sarah to conceive, and, at her advanced age, she gives birth to Isaac. So there are now two male children in Abraham's household, Sarah's son, Isaac, and Hagar's son, Ishmael.

The Torah tells us that Ishmael considers himself the family's legitimate heir. This means that, in addition to the household's wealth, Ishmael claims title to the spiritual legacy established by Abraham and Sarah. As the next patriarch, Ishmael would have been charged with continuing to spread the new monotheistic concept of Judaism. Sarah does not support Ishmael's ambitions.

She has great clarity with regard to his fundamental personality and foresees that he will eventually turn to idol worship, murder, and adultery. Later events prove her correct, but at the time Sarah alone perceives that Isaac should be the next patriarch and that Ishmael must be removed from the household. Only with the disappearance of Ishmael's negative influence will Isaac safely inherit the mantle of the fledgling Jewish nation.

Abraham strongly disagrees with Sarah's assessment. He is not yet ready to turn Ishmael out of the house — he sees no tangible proof of the boy's sinful character. Ishmael's true nature is clear only to Sarah. At this juncture, the Torah tells us that God intercedes on Sarah's behalf and commands Abraham to "listen to her voice in all that she tells you. It is through Isaac that you will gain posterity" (Genesis 21:12). In the end, owing to Sarah's foresight, the second generation of the Jewish people's forebears is secured.

Sarah's decision to banish Ishmael was not the result of favoritism toward Isaac, her biological son. Rather, it was intellectual preciseness — *binah* — which enabled Sarah to act decisively for the good of the Jewish nation.

Isaac continues his parents' work and eventually marries Rebecca, the next great matriarch, who again decides the course of Judaism. She gives birth to twins, Jacob and Esau. (Unlike Sarah before her, Rebecca is the biological mother of both sons.) Jacob becomes a scholar, Esau a hunter. Although the boys are very different, Isaac and Rebecca intend for them to work as a team toward the good of the Jewish people. In this regard, Jacob is supposed to oversee spiritual and intellectual growth, while Esau is charged with physical and material sustenance.

The Torah tells us that Isaac wants to give Esau a special blessing for material success. Rebecca, who is deeply in touch with the essential nature of Esau, can see past his current superficial righteousness and understands clearly what he will become. It is apparent to her that Esau will eventually use his father's blessing to undermine Jacob's scholarly pursuits, thus jeopardizing the future of Judaism. Rebecca sees that Jacob must become spiritually and materially independent of his brother. To this end, she orders Jacob to disguise himself as Esau in order to procure Isaac's powerful blessing. The plan works, and the Torah tells us that when Isaac discovers what has happened — and why — he acknowledges the righteousness of his wife's plan (Genesis 27:33). Without Rebecca's clarity, Judaism would have ended then and there.

Jacob takes his place as the third patriarch and marries two sisters, Rachel and Leah. The Torah tells us that Jacob, with his wives and children, lives and works for many difficult years in the house of his father-in-law, Laban. In spite of Laban's dishonest treatment, Jacob remains upright throughout his employment. God ultimately commands Jacob to return with his wives and children to the Land of Israel. At this turning point, Jacob — a man of peace — asks his wives' advice about whether to leave on good terms with Laban or whether they should depart abruptly (Genesis 31:4). Rachel and

Leah are aware that their father hopes to infect the young Jewish nation with his pagan ways, and they urge Jacob to sever all connections to Laban's household (Genesis 31:14). Jacob heeds their advice, and the family leaves under cover of darkness. Again, due to the insight of Rachel and Leah, Judaism progresses to its next stage of development, within the Land of Israel.

The matriarchs — Sarah, Rebecca, Rachel, and Leah — built the Jewish nation from within. Each woman possessed the ability to see what was not obvious to the patriarchs, and that is why there is a Jewish nation today. The trait of *binah* — the ability to analyze, distinguish, and thereby know the spiritual validity of something — requires tremendous effort and is, without exception, predicated on Torah knowledge. The Torah explains to us God's view of good and bad, finite and eternal, true and false — in other words, the value of all things we encounter. Then and now, Jewish women with a deep understanding of Torah use *binah* to categorize and understand new experiences and situations. Ultimately, female *binah* is meant to function as a searchlight of truth and clarity.

Every Jewish woman today is able to cultivate and excel in this aptitude. *Binah* is an inheritance of Jewish women and a gift to themselves, their families, their communities, and society as a whole.

ESTHER WEIN is a part-time instructor at the Jewish Renaissance Center in New York City, where she conducts classes in Jewish philosophy for women of little or no Jewish background. She also teaches a course entitled "Serious Questions You Always Wanted to Ask about Judaism" in several synagogues and two Long Island high schools, as well as a class on the weekly Torah portion in the White Shul. She resides in Lawrence, New York, with her husband, an attorney, and their four children.

Speaking about...
More Jewish Women,
Past

Great Jewish Women

J ewish tradition does not consider only those who were famous for their righteousness, generosity, or Torah knowledge worthy of the title "great." Fundamental to Jewish thought is the idea that God creates individuals with particular strengths meant for their self-development and the benefit of those around them. Most of us will never be famous, but still have crucial roles to fill for ourselves, our families, and others. Realizing one's potential is what makes a person truly great, whether or not historians ever notice it.

However, one way to learn how to actualize one's potential is by following another's example. Knowing about great women, then, can inspire us regarding the important roles Jewish women have had in our history, helping us carry out our responsibility to perpetuate a legacy of generations of Jewish women devoting themselves to Judaism and the Jewish people.

Deborah

Deborah was a great prophetess who served as a Judge of the Jewish people. When Israel was being attacked, the Jewish General Barak refused to wage war unless she joined him. She agreed and mobilized a huge army to defeat the enemy (see Judges, ch. 5). Deborah was also known for making the wicks for the torches in the Temple in order to encourage Torah learning. In the Bible she is called "Deborah, woman of torches," because this support of Torah is considered an even greater contribution to the future of the Jewish people than her military victories. With all her accomplishments, in the famous "Deborah's Song" she referred to herself as "a mother in Israel," because she saw motherhood as her greatest role.

Queen Shlomzion

Against her wishes, Shlomzion's (139–67 B.C.E.) husband, Alexander Yanneus, conducted a reign of terror against the Jewish populace, especially the Rabbis. She succeeded him and restored respect to Judaism, inviting Jewish scholars to return from exile and rebuilding yeshivot. A strictly observant Jew, she was outstanding in her devotion to Jewish teachings. Due to her great qualities, the entire Land of Israel was blessed, with fruits growing to great sizes. The Rabbis preserved some of these so that later generations would be inspired by the rewards of piety. Her reinvigoration of Jewish life enabled the Jewish people to survive the destruction of Jerusalem and the exile that soon followed.

Bruriah

Bruriah was a brilliant woman who is said to have learned three hundred Jewish laws a day. One of the most famous incidents concerning her is a sad one. Her two sons died on Shabbat, but she did not want to burden her husband Rabbi Meir during the joyous holy day, and so she delayed telling him. After nightfall, she asked him, "Sometime ago I was given something to enjoy, but now the one who gave it to me wants it back. Must I return it?" Surprised by the simple question, he responded affirmatively. Bruriah showed Rabbi Meir their dead sons. He began to weep and she asked, "Did you not tell me to return what was loaned? God gave, and God has taken away, blessed is God."

Ima Shalom

A Roman noble once visited Ima Shalom. He began to ridicule Judaism, claiming that it was preposterous to believe in a God who was a thief. Didn't he steal Adam's rib to create Eve?

Ima Shalom pretended to get angry and said, "I am going to the Roman ruler to seek justice. Last night a burglar stole my silver and left gold in its place."

The noble laughed. "Surely he is no thief but a friend."

Ima Shalom responded, "So it is with our God. He took a single rib from Adam, of little use, and returned a most valuable gift: a partner, a wife."

The Roman pressed on. "If so, why did your God seem ashamed of it and put Adam to sleep before taking the rib?"

Ima Shalom summoned her servant and ordered him to go to the market and return with fresh meat. Upon his return, she spiced and prepared the meat before the Roman's eyes. When it was ready, she offered him a piece, but he refused. "I cannot enjoy the dish, for I still think of it in its raw, distasteful state of a little while ago."

Ima Shalom explained, "So it was with Adam and Eve. He was put to sleep in order to be able to appreciate her for beauty and not be a witness to her formation." (This story is based on Talmud, *Sanhedrin* 39.)

Donna Gracia Mendes

The persecutions in fifteenth-century Spain left

hundreds of thousands of Jews dead and many more homeless and wandering. Many became *conversos*, outwardly leading Christian lives while secretly practicing Judaism. Discovery was extremely dangerous.

Donna Gracia was born into such a family and was in charge of a large banking empire. The Belgian king tried to confiscate the bank's holdings by claiming she was a hidden Jew. She cunningly avoided the charge and managed to get her family and her wealth into the Ottoman Empire. There she shed her Christian exterior and became a valiant leader of the Jewish people, using her wealth to provide for the needy, build synagogues, and give stipends to Torah scholars, enabling them to focus completely on their studies. When the Christians in Ancona burned twenty-four Jews at the stake, Donna Gracia organized the first modern boycott to punish the city, setting a precedent that inspired much community action for future generations. Through her piety, meticulous observance of Jewish law, and leadership, she won the respect and admiration of the entire Jewish people and became known as the "Esther of her time."

Gluckel of Hameln

Gluckel of Hameln was not particularly famous during her lifetime in seventeenth-century Germany. How do we know of her at all? She wrote memoirs, partly in consolation over the loss of her dear husband, Chaim.

She writes how the Jews had to fear antisemitic mobs, and "every woman thanked God when she saw her husband safe after each business day." Gluckel writes proudly how her husband had fixed times for Torah study, prayed with fervor, and treated his wife with great love and respect. She was his partner and main adviser in all his commercial endeavors.

Her deep faith is clear in her writing, as is her meticulous observance of Jewish law. Not only is her book full of exhortations to improve our ways, but she also instructs her children how they may best serve God. It is through her profound beliefs and dedication to living an authentic Jewish life that Gluckel, like most unknown men and women in Jewish history, was truly great.

The Maid of Ludmir

Channa Rachel Werbermacher, who lived in the nineteenth century, was known as the "Maid of Ludmir." She applied herself assiduously from a young age to become well educated in Torah and prayed with unusual devotion.

Once, upon visiting her mother's grave, she collapsed and fell into a coma. She explained to her father that she had visited Heaven and received a new soul. The great Reb Mordechai of Chernobyl substantiated her claim saying, "We do not know whose religious soul is dwelling in this woman." With this recognition, she took on new prominence.

She eventually moved to the Land of Israel, and, together with an elderly kabbalist, was intent on a course of action they understood would bring the Messiah. A meeting was set, but as her partner was leaving his home, a poor wayfarer came to the door asking for food and comfort. The meeting was subsequently missed. chassidic lore explains that the wayfarer was Elijah the prophet, who interfered because the world was not yet ready for the Messiah.

Grace Aguilar

An English Jew living in the nineteenth century, Grace Aguilar was deeply observant and a well-known writer, most of her work being about Judaism and Israel.

She wrote mostly to women, inspiring them to learn more about Judaism and realize the beauty in being a traditional Jewish woman.

She published her most famous work, *The Spirit of Judaism: In Defense of Her Faith and Its Professors*, when she was only twenty-one. Her next work, *The Jewish Faith: Its Spiritual Consolation, Moral Guidance, and Immortal Hope*, was published soon after, as were many of her novels.

She died at the young age of thirty-one, yet in her short life she helped hundreds of women realize their important and dignified place in Judaism. Before her death, more than one hundred women who had been influenced by her wrote to her. They said: "You, dearest sister...have taught us to know and appreciate our dignity, to feel and prove that no female character can be...more pure than that of the Jewish maiden, none more pious than that of the women in Israel. You have vindicated our social and spiritual equality with our brethren in the faith; you have, by your own excellent example, triumphantly refuted the aspersion that the Jewish religion leaves unmoved the heart of the Jewish woman...."

Sarah Schenirer

A seamstress living in early twentieth-century Poland, Sarah Schenirer had a profound and invaluable effect on Jewish women. After centuries of pogroms, persecution, and poverty, Jewish learning had drastically declined. Only a small percentage of Jewish men had any real knowledge of their heritage. Women's education was even more neglected. For lack of alternatives, young women from traditional homes attended nonreligious schools and were led away from Judaism.

Greatly disturbed by the situation, Sarah Schenirer

cried out, "Watch how the girls pray — without motivation, as if it were forced upon them. Some are here to
please their parents; others, as if God needs their
prayers. My sisters! When will you understand that our
main purpose for being on this earth is to serve God?"

A bright and warm-hearted woman, Sarah Schenirer
understood that those who left Judaism did so out of ig-
norance. She wished to show them the great beauty and
depth of the Jewish tradition. Leading rabbis blessed her
endeavors and wished her success.

In 1918, Sarah Schenirer opened her first school
starting with twenty-five girls. The girls loved learning
about their heritage and religion, and more joined.
Within a short time, Bais Yaakov schools opened all
over Europe, and she founded a teachers' seminary to
fill the need for educators. By 1937, there were two hundred and fifty Bais Yaakovs with thirty-eight thousand
students throughout eastern and central Europe, along
with youth organizations and summer camps. Today it
is the largest Jewish women's educational system in the
world.

Chaya Feldman

Chaya Feldman lived during that recent, tragic time
in our history — the Holocaust. She was a student of Sarah Schenirer and taught us about the ultimate self-
sacrifice of Sarah Schenirer's girls. We will let Chaya
Feldman tell you their story:

"...By the time you receive this letter, I will no longer be alive. In another few hours, we will all be part of
history. We are ninety-three girls, ages fourteen
through twenty-two, living in four rooms. On the
twenty-seventh of July, a contingent of the Gestapo
forcibly removed us from our rooms and threw us into a
dark dungeon. We were given only water to drink, and

the young girls were terribly frightened. The only words of comfort I can offer them is that in a short while we will once again be with our mother Sarah Schenirer.

"Yesterday they took us from this dark room, removed all our clothing, and washed us, leaving us only one single tunic each as a covering. They told us that today the German soldiers would be coming to visit us. We immediately agreed upon a suicide pact. The Germans do not know that the bath we were given was our ritual immersion prior to our death. We all possess poison that we set aside for just such an emergency. When the soldiers begin to arrive, we intend to drink this poison. We spent today saying *vidui*, uttering our last confessions. We are not afraid. We have only one request: Please say Kaddish for ninety-three Jewish women."

This Great Jewish Women section was compiled by LISA STEVENSEN, who wishes to thank the Heritage House Free Jewish Youth Hostel for Women in the Old City of Jerusalem and Chabad Houses around the world for their warmth and meaningful Jewish connections. For more biographies of great Jewish women, visit us at www.jewishmatters.com.

HELPING PUT CONTENT INTO CONTINUITY

OUR PEOPLE
Natan Lopes Cardozo
Ken Spiro
Shraga Simmons
Michael Skobac

OUR LIFE
Judy Auerbach
Rivkah Slonim
Eli Gewirtz
Mordechai Becher
Holly Pavlov
Gila Manolson
Yirmiyohu and
Tehilla Abramov

Denah Weinberg
Lynn Finson
Tzippora Heller
Avraham Edelstein
Leah Kohn

OUR G-D
Lawrence Kelemen
Ellen Solomon
Dovid Gottlieb
Gerald Schroeder
Lisa Aiken
Dovid Orlofsky

With more and more Jews interested in rediscovering their heritage, here's a little book with answers to some very big questions. Twenty-four renowned philosophers, writers, educators, rabbis, and scientists share their insights, wisdom, and experience on issues as varied as Shabbat observance, Big Bang theory, and feminism and Judaism. *Jewish Matters* is an essential tool for searching Jews — and for anyone who wants to help them on their wonderful voyage of rediscovery.

A TARGUM PRESS Book
Distributed by Feldheim Publishers

Coming soon in the
Jewish Matters series

JEWISH HOLIDAY MATTERS

and

JEWISH LIFECYCLE MATTERS

For excerpts, reviews, to be in touch with
our contributors, or just to let us know how
you liked the book, please visit us at

www.jewishmatters.com

We look forward
to hearing from you!